DIGGING OUT OF DISTRACTION:

Butt In Chair, Hands on Keys on the Road to Publication

CHRISTINE GLOVER

Digging Out of Distraction: Butt In Chair, Hands On Keys On the Road to Publication © 2015 Christine Glover

Edited by: Heidi Scribner

Cover by: Mallory Glover

Formatting by <u>Sweet 'N Spicy Designs</u>

<u>www.christinegloversite.com</u>

ISBN: 978-1517132255

Here's to making all our dreams and wishes come true! Never give up and never surrender—stay on course and you will arrive at your destination!

Excerpt

No matter where we are in our careers or on this journey, we will always have mountains standing in our way. We will always have boulders in our path blocking our passage, and we will always have rivers to navigate to get to the other side. The trick is doing it. Doing it in spite of the worry, the fear, the doubts, the concerns, and the possibility of failing. The trick is to believe that the mountain can be climbed, the boulder can be moved out of the way, and the river can be navigated safely.

The courage to face the fear and do it anyway is not in all of us. But it is in some of us. Even that courage doesn't mean success. Not outwardly. But it does mean success within. The knowledge of one's fortitude is success. How many times did Rocky get hit? How many times did we fight any enemy nation and think we'd lose? But we did it anyway. We performed.

The trick is to keep working and performing despite the obstacles in our way. The trick is to keep working and performing even when no one comes to watch the show.

That is the hardest lesson to learn. When we have only an audience of one, we still have to perform.

BICHOK: Butt in Chair, Hands On Keys

Dear Heidi,
Thank you for your love, support & enjoying friendship!
You are a light in my life!
XXOO -
Christine

A Form of Distraction

November 16, 2008

Today I started a new blog, one to distract, yet motivate me to write more—focus consistently. Lessons I've learned from other writers in the past week include.

- 100 words a day, every day.
- set a timer (this really works... no play until timer chimes) I set the microwave to 60 minutes and write until it beeps, take a break, and then reset to 60 minutes.
- Set writing goals: weekly/daily.
- Enter contests to set artificial deadlines.

So if you're stuck, want to get unstuck, set the timer, promise yourself a page, and move forward. It's hard to write in a vacuum of no pay, no recognition. Self-discipline is the key.

Writing through Moods

November 18, 2008

I'll be the first to admit that when I am tired, cranky, frustrated, angry, or all the above, I find it difficult to focus. Today is one of those days.

But, I have a deadline. I cannot let this situation overtake my motivation and derail my focus.

So how do I push through the inner distraction demons?

Some ways I will cope today are:

- Venting to get it out of my system.
- Coffee, coffee, coffee.
- Use the timer religiously.
- Avoid other websites until I am finished writing for the day.
- Take Motrin.
- Work out to clear out the cobwebs in my brain.
- Remind myself that whatever someone else's problem is, it is just that... someone else's problem.

Moods are a part of life. I can't let a mood stand in the way of my goals.

Writing through Illness

December 5, 2008

When I 'worked' outside the home, I'd push through a cold and go into the office if I didn't have a fever. I did this even if my nose felt like a train ran through it or I was in pain. But now, as a writer struggling to get published, I am asking myself, is it worth feeling miserable with a dripping nose? No one is paying me, and no one cares if I show up to the computer keyboard. But then I reminded myself that I care.

So even though I spent the better part of last night blowing my nose and feeling like crapola, and even though my nose is drippier than a leaky faucet, I am going to write for at least one hour today.

Of course, who knows what those wonderful cold medications will do to my ability to string together two words or a paragraph???

A Cat on My Lap and A Day to Refocus

December 16, 2008

I think I've discovered that the weather really distracts me from writing. It's rainy and cold out there and all I want to do is hunker beneath the covers and read a book. Writing? Bah humbug. And I have a ton of goodies still to make... by myself because my daughter is swamped with schoolwork and finals and recitals and the list goes on.

How will I ever do even one hour today? But I will.

The only thing suffering is my exercise routine. I joined a gym to go workout there on crappy days like this—group fitness starts at 8:30am. But I haven't gone since the week before Thanksgiving because the day just sucks if I break up my morning. The main reason I joined was to make new friends. Ha. That hasn't happened. Nobody really talks there. One person did approach me, but it was to give me a pointer on how to stomp more quietly on my step ... so much for making new friends. She didn't even give me her name first!

Maybe that is why I am not going to that gym.

Or maybe I am just a *lazy von lazerson* type person because I am tired, I have a sinus infection, and all I want to do is sleep on cold, nasty, rainy days. The fact that I write at all at this point is already a minor miracle.

So, grumpy and tired and lazy to boot am I. But I will write my hour today. I will!

Procrastination Anyone?

April 4, 2009

I guess the wind blew out of my sails pretty hard when I didn't final in the GH (Golden Heart contest for unpublished writers). I've blown air into them a few times and managed to read through the MS (manuscript), and work on my character workshop. Other than that, I've spent the majority of my time trolling through blogs, playing on Facebook, reading taglines on websites, planning business cards, and fritzing around.

I simply haven't been focused.

I know that it is okay. That down time is fine as long as I inject some effort into the actual process of writing. But I am in a bit of a limbo as I am waiting to hear back from my CP (critique partner) about the last eighty pages of the book and I am in a class in which I have only focused on one character.

What to do about it? I think I will impose the timer rule.

One hour on writing and half an hour off for the rest of the day until 4:00pm. I have company coming for dinner, the usual household chores and cleaning, baking, and more that I want to accomplish. The writing will be my work, the other stuff my break.

This will be in place until Monday. Then I will have to start working on the global fixes in my book.

Nurturing My Writing Voice

May 23, 2009

I am in the midst of my revision for book three. I feel like I've been dealing with these people forever. But with each new revision or change, I find I like the book more and more.

Part of this is the discovery of craft—the tools and techniques used to write a story—and learning to polish my writing. Another part is taking the Book-In-A-Week class, which helped me rediscover how to develop my story and my unique way of getting into my characters' heads. The final part of this is through reading some amazing new books published by fellow writers I respect and admire. There, sometimes, the rules of craft and contest are blurred because the story is the key.

I LOVE THESE BOOKS!!

I only read other books at night, or when I am on vacation, right before beddie-bye. If I read them during the day, I will lose precious writing time. Right now I am on a mission! I must finish the next seven chapters in revision in seven allotted writing days. Then I get to dive into my fourth novel and play around with those wonderful people (who are starting to get very impatient with my constant dabbling with book three).

The flow of the words in the books I read has infiltrated my own writing; not as an exact duplication, but in the idea of how my characters think, act, talk to themselves, and face the world. In that world, overused words are, well, allowed, and echoes can occur, and *ly* words exist, and *was* isn't a demon word.

Thus my inner critic is silenced to allow my people to become who they are: internally.

Love that feeling.

The writing is tighter. No doubt about it. The weaving in and out of elements is more precise. I like the new flow. Will it appeal to an editor or an agent? I don't know. But I do know it appeals to the deeper part in me who enjoys reading a well-crafted romance with a fabulous hero, though flawed, and an independent heroine who's itching for a bit of subduing.

It's like first draft writing, but it's a tighter blend of writing for self, writing for the reader or critique group, and writing for the editor who might one day request it and then accept it with the codicil: more revision required.

I'm determined to move forward with this book. I want to pitch it at the conference. I am ready to try to sell the work. If no one asks for it, I'll try elsewhere via queries. Then I will lovingly set it aside and use what I've learned by writing it in all my future novels as well as in other revisions.

This is why I love to write. It challenges me, it changes me, and it moves me beyond preset boundaries. I've learned that it is quite all right to be a "delusional masochist" while pursuing this grand obsession.

The Three Ps of Writing Cooked Up Three Ways

December 4, 2009

Writer Speak—we all get better at it the longer we're in the game. Lately, I've noticed a strange synchronicity between some of my favorite triple play letters. I call them PPPs.

What does PPP mean? In writer speak it is short for Pivotal Plot Point. This is a part of the book where the main characters must make a decision that leads them to growth (ultimately), but there are a lot of consequences with each PPP. There are all these different terms for it like Twist Point, Turning Point, and more. Big PPPs include the inevitable Black Moment, or Point of No Return and finally the Climax. PPPs are important parts of the book's plot. Without them, there's no reason to turn the page. That's my quick and dirty dictionary explanation. I know there are plenty of books out there that give better definitions, but that's how I see them. PPPs. Can't write without them.

My second group of PPPs occurs after a rejection (or R in writer speak), small or large. Some rejections are easier to bear than others. But none are pleasant. As a writer, when I get one, I throw me a little PPP. That's dejected writer speak for Personal Pity Party. This is my 24 hour period of mourning time where I get to drink copious amounts of wine, sing Eighties pop music, refuse to cook meals, wallow in self-pity and doubt, question my course of direction, whine to my CPs (ooh another P—Partner) about the difficulties we all face in this insane writing world, take a break from writing and basically allow myself time to mourn the R. Rs suck. Period. The. End. I just threw myself a PPP.

But my party time is drawing to a close. I have reached the Twenty-four hour mark. Now it is time to quit wallowing and start working again. Actually, during part of this R's PPP, I did work. I sent off two more queries to agencies I love and I sent off an unsolicited query to my target publisher. Same house; different editor. May as well see which way the chips fall for this book one way or another. So a bit of action—kind of my mini-denial/anger/kick it back phase. I even looked at the WIP (Work In Progress). For about a Nano second. Wrote it off as a "to do tomorrow" and I'm having a positive interaction and real dinner party tonight with friends who care nothing about writing and only care about me, the person.

This brings me to what separates a writer with chutzpah from one who can't take it on the chin. It sucks to get punched in the solar plexus. It does, but you won't get published at all until you take those punches. Did you know only 20% of authors who pitch and get requests at conferences actually send in their requested materials? Why is that? Part of it might be the MS isn't finished or not even started. What about those who are finished? Why don't they send it in? Fear. It's scary to send your book baby out into the universe. We've heard the stories. More rejections are received than requests and contracts.

Who wants to have their bubble burst with that kind of pain? Me. I do. I want to get rejected because it means I am attempting very hard to get published. So perseverance is important. Never give up and never surrender. Also, a person needs patience. Some people hit the bulls-eye first time out. Most people don't. Don't throw away your dream or short change it because you can't wait for the eventual success. Be patient. Keep working. Keep moving forward. That leads to Persistence. We must be persistent. We must write. We must improve our craft. We must submit and pitch and risk rejection over and over again. Otherwise, we'll never get there.

I can't predict if, or when, someone is going to look at what I've written and say, *wow, we really need to give that fabulous writer a contract* (really why hasn't anyone done so yet—this is me in my denial mode again—it does help). So don't give up, be patient with your dream and risk rejection. It's the only way you'll achieve your goals.

Brain Freeze

January 4, 2010

It's cold outside. For this part of the country that's unusual. Man, I didn't even venture out to the curb to get a newspaper. I must confess, my creative juices were thick, ice-cold blocks that failed to melt today. No way. In addition to the cold, frigid, nasty wind and future predictions of snow freezing my brain cells, I also had the Teen home all day.

Rather than fight the ennui and the lack of motivation, I focused on calling a dear friend before the hustle and bustle truly kicks in. Then I organized my writing space, and then I picked up Donald Maass's book *Writing the Breakout Novel* and read through the foreword by Anne Perry, the introduction by Maass and the first chapter.

I'm determined to read the book and just absorb the info as I work on the 3rd revision. One thing that was nice to read was Anne Perry runs through her books at least 4-5 times. And it's as painful for her to do it as it is for me. But she said she knew her story's heart and that remained the same. That also inspired me. Does this mean that I believe I have a breakout novel in my house right now? Heck no. I have what's seriously a break-my-brain novel in my house right now. But what I love is that true writing, real to the guts writing, the kind that sells, boils down to Telling A Story, and telling it well.

I have a story. I want to tell it well. I want to make it sing. I'm encouraged that to get the heart of my story out there into the world, I'll have to break my own heart to write it. Cutting scenes and pasting them and dumping them and rewriting scenes and creating deeper plot points and weaving all the elements into the story will take time.

I will commit the time. I will write my peeps' story. I will write it to the best of my ability as I grow and learn the craft.

Is this *The Book*? *shoulder shrug* I don't know. But I know it is *my story*, and I will write it for my peeps. The rest is up to the Gods... and truthfully, Maass reiterated the one thing I already knew: I only have control over one thing. That is writing the story. In a way, that gives me hope that I have control over my destiny.

You know, I did say one has to be a bit delusional to write. I guess I will hang onto my delusions.

Muffin Top Middle

February 8, 2010

I am currently revising my dreaded middle section of the WIP. Let me repeat: dreaded middle section.

Now for the non-writers out there or for the writers who only make it to the middle of a novel, lose heart and quit, here is a truism: writing through the middle section of a WIP/First Draft and a WIP/In Revision for the Billionth Time is painful and soul-sucking work. This is not for the faint of heart. Nope. One must forge ahead, knowing the maps and outlines created to prevent this mind-numbing process have failed. Or at least we believe they have and we would love to kill the characters and move on.

Confession: According to my loving CP in Virginia, I whine a lot as I enter into this phase.

As I grit my teeth and buckle down to wrestle the horrible plot into shape, I begin to have hope and become somewhat euphoric because I can see the solutions unfolding and bringing me to new lands. I don't kill my peeps, they find a great way to fix life's many problems, the villain or bad dude is conquered and all the loose threads are neatly tucked into a bow.

It's a glimmer of hope. One that will ebb when I have to tighten the writing, but it can be done.

Confession: I don't know of a single writer, published or unpublished, who doesn't go through the *I suck* period while stuck in the middle of their MS.

I'm muddling along with my current WIP in Revision while nursing the Physicist (AKA my husband) through his hip replacement recovery and all that entails. While not trying to squeeze in writing time, I am reading Maass' book, *Writing the Breakout Novel*. A few days ago, while waiting for the Physicist to get through his surgery, I read the following:

"Breakout novels sprawl... it can be a scary prospect, this business of writing large. In mid-manuscript a breakout novelist can feel lost, overwhelmed by possible scenes and the challenge of tying up every thread... it is common for outlines to breakdown... many breakout novelists realize they have not looked at their outline in months... instead they are pushing forward on instinct, using some inner sense of direction to keep them driving toward the high moments and, eventually, the final line."

This is where I am-the midsection. It's growing into a muffin top midsection. Yet I persist because I sort of envision the final destination for my peeps. The story is taking a life of its own. I love this part of the writing process. It's not going fast, but it is going well. I know it will need a lot of shining and polishing when it's done, but oh the plotting and playing with it is fabulous.

My midsection is a muffin top.

What is a muffin top? It's that top of the muffin that spills over the ends of the cupcake holder and makes a lovely half moon shape. It's got all the ingredients inside it and when one bites into it, sheer delight.

Confession: Not only is my midsection of the MS a muffin top, my belly is currently a muffin top spilling over my jeans due to a long cold winter, too many hours of BICHOK and not enough hours trimming the middle down through diet and exercise.

That is what I am getting ready to do—put my MS on a diet and exercise program. I will whip this puppy into shape using whatever means I can to get the story told.

Meanwhile, pass the muffins.

K.I.S.S. & Tell

February 16, 2010

Revision is an interesting process. I've discovered that when it comes to the PLOT revision, reading a writing craft book alongside the writing work helps me to generate new ideas and fix my MS's holes. Sometimes I take a course online during this time. Sometimes I just read and learn.

While revising, I am always on the phone or pinging emails to my CPs. They are all working on their WIPs and going through the same process. All of our voices bring new thoughts and solutions to the table. All of us find different ways to get to the heart of the matter.

So where is the KISS?

It's in the phrase: Keep It Simple Silly. The more I learn, the more I realize that writing does boil down to basics. There are some amazing methods to approach writing, but they all derive from similar roots. I can call a plot point a twist point, a pivotal plot point, a false victory, a turning point... a whatever... But bottom line: the idea is the same. I have to have sections in my book that bring about changes internally and externally to my main characters and all of these changes must deepen the sympathy my future readers have for my characters.

Goals? Motivations? Conflicts? Internal and external? They all come from some deep well within ourselves. If we don't mine our own hearts and experiences, we aren't bringing an honest revelation to the table, either. At times it takes some wonderful teacher to lead us to that discovery. Other times, it's an aha moment within our own brains that crystalizes the soul baring drive to write the story. Is our theme throughout our writing about betrayal, hope, lost souls finding home, overcoming injustice, saving people, truth and justice overcoming dishonesty? What? When we discover this, we are on a roll.

Sounds simple doesn't it?

But that's the part that's hard to tell. When does the writing shift from complex to simple? When does the book take on an amazing life of its own where the characters are really telling me how to write their story? I think it happens all along, as long as I don't force the issue. As soon as I try to fake it, I lose it.

I lose the essence of my people. I lose the essence of their story.

Revision opens up new pathways, new directions, new goals. Revision brings along interesting developments, unexpected characters and evocative emotions. Now the question is are you ready to expose them to the light?

Finished? Nope. I Need an Extra Helping

March 3, 2010

Ah, once again I reach the end of this crazy WIP. Oh, the joy. Oh, the rhapsody. Oh, the knowledge that this is not goodbye... but until we meet again. Yes, I know I am *finished*. But I am not done. Not by a long shot.

For I see in the ending, a new way to write the beginning, the middle and the end again.

Let me begin by saying that this current WIP has been an interesting journey. I started in February 2009. I wrote the first draft in a week. Yes. You read it here. A WEEK! 50,000 words! I planned for it during a class and prepped for 3 weeks before I hacked out 50K in a week.

I loved my original premise for the story. Loved my own motivation for writing the story. The motivation is what keeps me going. The premise? It's the same, but oh, so different in approach.

You see. It started as a story targeting a specific line for a specific category. A short Contemporary Romance. Now it is morphing into something much more. Not a category. Not a specific line. Not anything more than an exploration of two unique characters.

These characters, my hero and heroine, are why I have battled to save the story. For it's changed. Not just because I am transforming it from a category length to a single title length, but what began as a fun romp has transformed into a deeper exploration of their psyches. And, therefore, by default, a deeper mining of my own psyche.

Now some of this transformation occurred during a bizarre soul searching period where I revisited my own painfully emotional historical landscape. Oh joy. Woohoo. Loved that. All of it brought about by one note. One request. That forced me to reexamine my past works and realize that I had denied a very important part of ME in the writing.

Oh, time to mine the heart. Thanks to Donald Maass, I realized I had to dig very deep and unveil more aspects of myself than I had intended. Wow. But I did. Now I know those revelations will have to be explored again, earlier in the WIP than they are now.

But they are there!

I can cut and weave them into the story earlier.

I wasn't worried about the sequential unfolding of story as much as I was concerned about the characters revealing even more of themselves to me. Wow, they are so strong, so giving, and so proud. I love them and I've decided that even if they aren't marketable, they are special.

By writing their story, I am bringing myself closer to writing better.

That is the goal of my journey.

Revelation. To. Oneself.

Separation Anxiety

March 11, 2010

Now that I have printed out my hard copy of the WIP in Revision, I need to let it sit on the shelf for a week or so. Why? Right now I can't see the forest for the trees. My brain needs a break. I need to shift my focus and look in another direction for a while in order to come back to the WIP with a fresh mind. I also need to take a break because I need to be receptive to the critiques I'll be getting from my CPs. I might want to rebel, but the truth is, I need to look at my "baby" with a critical eye.

But separating oneself from a WIP one's worked on for four months is tough. Here are some ways that I handle the separation anxiety:

1. Try to finish the WIPs, writing work before a major holiday or break. In this case, Spring Break starts on Saturday. Now I'm gearing up for the break, a trip and getting excited about seeing my friends in North Carolina.

2. Plan to exchange work with my CPs. This way I can fill my need to read, but it's my CP's work and it takes me out of my writing world.

3. Read a writing craft book or take an online course while taking a break. This is a great way to prep for the next first draft and/or to brainstorm for ideas for the current WIP under Wraps.

4. Putter around the house. Do things I don't normally have time to do. Plan a gardening project or home project. Direct my creative energy elsewhere.

5. Catch up on my to-be-watched list (television or movies)

6. Plan fun events with my friends. Go for lunches. Shop. Visit cool places.

7. Catch up on my to-be-read pile (that stack of books I WANT to read that's next to my bed). Fill my mind with other people's amazing, published works.

8. Celebrate the fact that I've finished another wrestling round with the WIP.

9. Straighten up the office, the work space, clear out the old clutter and free myself for the next round or starting a new project.

10. Do nothing at all—don't have deadlines or schedules to meet. Just chillax and put my feet up. Rest is good for the creative soul.

Ripping Out Word Weeds

April 8, 2010

The hardest part about revising is the desire to add words and having to wait. Yes, wait. Sure, I've got the first global pass on the total WIP and I've managed to fix a couple of big picture problems more easily than I had anticipated which is a relief. I've even got some fabulous ideas about how to make this a bigger, lighter book with the depth it needs to go to a single title.

But I can't act on the ideas because I'm not finished weeding out the words I don't need. I am editing out the darker elements I had in the book and layering in lighter touches and/or marking the scene to do so at another time. I am also noting where I need to add scenes, and I am writing down all my brainstorming ideas into my trusty notebook. I have to be patient as I work through the scenes I've already written otherwise a good idea might not be useful OR I won't know where to place my new scenes and my revised scenes.

It's like gardening. First you have to pull the weeds, plow the dirt and add the fertilizer before you can plant the seeds for new growth. That's what I am doing. Some writers give up at this point and move on to writing a new MS because the task is overwhelming. Then they might return to their WIP in revision and be able to work on it, but I can't work that way. That would be like planting seeds for a new garden next to a weedy patch. Then the weeds in the old garden might overrun my new garden.

What would be the point? I'd have another weedy garden to fix.

Oddly enough, I had hoped to play with my new YA idea this week, but by the time I finish working all day on my revision, I have nothing left to draw from my creative well. All my energy is going into the revision. I'm not fighting it. I believe that if I do have a spark for the other idea, then I'll run with it. My brain will know when it is ready to work on something different.

I've been down this revision path before. It's murky at times. MS number three took over a year to wrestle into shape. The book did get better with each revision, but the revising didn't get easier. Even at the very end of number three's revision, I went through it and picked out details that needed strengthening or finessing. Now I can play around with it to change the minor details and keep my mind focused on the fourth MS, but I don't think I could work on a first draft of a new story without draining my creative energy. And I need my creativity to stay true to the task at hand.

I imagine published authors work on more than one book at a time, but I wonder if that is after they've really gutted a story and revised it. Line editing and tweaking is not revising. Revising is getting into the heart of the story and rearranging the way the story is pumped out.

I know I can't revise this fourth MS forever. I need to get it to a point where I can say I'm as done as I can be and move on. I've given myself until the end of June. Maybe I'll finish earlier. Maybe I won't. I do know that I need a partial and a synopsis by June 1st for the MAGGIES®—a prestigious contest for unpublished and published writers coordinated by the Georgia Romance Writers®— regardless of where the rest of the MS stands. Afterward, I need to know that the book I'm pitching has a solid plot, and that the bones and muscles of this book are set and grounded. Then it'll be easier to fine-tune the story should an editor or agent request the full.

Twist, Turn, Pivot and Point: Structure & Plot

April 9, 2010

I'm nearly ready to transfer my entire document back into a new project in the Scrivener© program. I love this program. I can easily shift my scenes around, mark my structure points, color code my hero/heroine/villain cards and more. Oh, it is a lovely writing tool.

Before I move my WIP into Scrivener©, I am revisiting the idea of plot and structure. I've read a few books on the subject and they've helped me clarify the major points I need to work toward in my overall novel writing. However, at times they merely muddy my thinking because there are about twenty billion different ways to label the major turning points and sections of the novel. Many novels and commercial movies have been dissected using these amazing templates.

I am in awe of any writer who can sit down with any novel idea/template and know all the answers before she starts writing.

I am not that kind of a writer.

I know most of the answers, or think I know. Then I write away and try to meet the goals I've set for my writing. Then I read my muddled mess, or send it to CPs or enter contests or share it a workshops, and all my clever plotting and ideas are shot down (not all, but a lot or they are asked to go to the next level—whatever that is as I don't often know what my original level is).

Then I sit down, rip out the parts that aren't working, or don't resonate, and try to come up with more answers to the original questions and fill in renewed blank spaces that I thought were answered. Finally, I have to look at the mess again and try to create order out of my chaos.

So here I am at the apex of binding my WIP into a solid structure and I am revisiting the plotting ideas once more.

This time I am reading the book Story Structure-Demysefiedby Larry Brooks. He's really good at distilling the information for the reader. The book is a fast read (thank goodness), and it offers really amazing examples from movies like Titanic and books like The Davinci Code. He renames some of the points, restructures some of the elements I've gleaned, but essentially I already have the basics written down on my handy dandy chapter/scene skeleton outline (it is very simplistic).

Sure, the words are different (not all, but some), but it is basically the same. So even though I have had this skeleton and have used it for every revision, guess what? Yeah, you got it—I still have to rip the guts out of the story. I haven't quite nailed down all the plot points/major milestones, or I have them but they're not in the right spots.

What gets me is that the information is essentially the same, but the labels become different. For instance, Inciting Incident. That's Larry's Hook. His Inciting Incident is the First Plot Point. Or in another language The First Pivotal Plot Point. He talks about the 3 Act Structure in terms of the novel and screenwriting, but for the novel, he talks about 4 Boxes. And what scenes belong in each Box. And his Orphan, Wanderer, Warrior, Martyr remind me of the hero's mythical journey (or something like that—I have that info tucked somewhere).

I'm glad he does re-label or restate the facts in a new way for me. Why? It makes me think outside of my box. I start brainstorming and getting new ideas for my book. I am affirmed about what is working for me as a writer, organically and structurally. I'd love to become the writer he talks about. You know, the writer that figures out all the points, the main items in the boxes, and then writes a fairly clean first draft where it needs only minor revisions.

Heck, that's why I read structure books. They give me hope that one day I won't need to gut my stories four, five or more times. But the truth is, I'll be lucky if I can get away with not gutting more than twice. That's my goal. At least until I get the "call" and an editor asks me to gut my story and revise it again.

So here are the fun ways to label plot points and story arcs I've gleaned over the years I've been struggling with structure:

- TWIST POINTS
- PINCH POINTS
- PIVOTAL PLOT POINTS
- INCITING INCIDENT
- OPENING HOOK
- MID POINT
- FALSE VICTORY
- CALL TO ACTION
- THIRD PLOT POINT
- FALSE DEFEAT
- CLIMAX
- RESOLUTION
- ACT 1
- ACT 2
- ACT 3
- BOXES
- SET UP
- RESPONSE
- ATTACK
- RESOLUTION
- BEGINNING
- MIDDLE
- END
- BLACK MOMENT
- ROMANTIC BLACK MOMENT
- POINT OF NO RETURN
- ALL IS LOST
- PANTSER

- PLOTTER
- MIST

You get the picture. Is it any wonder I consider my writing process organized chaos?

Writers, WIPs, Wrangling & Work

April 20, 2010

I'm back from my workshop in Atlanta, but I am not jumping back into my writing. Why? The answers I sought only led to more questions about my story. I am glad I went to the all day workshop, but now I must examine my story a bit more closely and make sure that my plot is strong enough.

Intuitively I already knew my story had plotting issues. This is what happens when you don't shore up all the lovely scenes in your head with solid structure points. Every time I go back into the story to fix a major plot point, it affects the entire story. As one writer friend said, it's like pushing down a domino and then a whole row tumbles.

I know my beginning, my set up, my ending and my pinch points. But the middle is a bit iffy. I believe it's a decent midpoint, but I brought the middle to the workshop to make sure it was decent.

The leaders said I needed more. A bigger reason for why my heroine wants to do what she does. I need a very compelling reason for her decision to stay in the area she is living in. But I balk now at the idea of adding a HUGE plot element to fix the story. Why? Another author who critiqued my work said to "keep it simple." There will be "more than enough conflict" to compel the reader to read.

I've brainstormed fun ideas to shore up the story with one CP. Suddenly I am on the Internet researching Burlesque dancing (don't ask—long story). Another CP said, "If the writing is compelling, the reader will read it anyway and why does anyone read the books they read?" Back to keeping it simple, right?

Repeat after me: writing isn't for sissies or the faint of heart.

In the meantime, I got contest entries back for my opening. I scored well. My *writing voice* was strong and they scored me high in that regard. Whew. One problem solved. I didn't final, but I didn't expect to as the story was still in major revision at the time I entered. I sent in the first ten pages to see if I was going in the right direction before an author told me that I had a two-tone story. I've worked my little writer fingers to the bone to fix the tone, but that was before the entry flew to the coordinator.

I was pleased that the comments and scores were pretty decent. Lots of perfect scores from two judges, one of the judges (a published author in romance so gotta heed that one) marked me low on my characterization and the other two marked me high. Two loved the original plot, but the author was iffy on the originality (there are only twelve stories in the world, the trick is to tell them in unique ways). The plot is different now, but that's okay. The issues with the characterization will be cleared up by fixing the tone.

Right, so now I have even more information to digest and deal with before I trudge onward. I eagerly (not) await my other contest scores (I know I didn't final because they called the finalists on Sunday and I didn't get a call). That entry was the same entry I sent to the critique author and had been changed already. I'm sure that one will not do well—I am praying for decent and constructive feedback.

Repeat after me: not all contest judges strive to be constructive and some of them are soul crushing critics who may not realize the pain they inflict isn't necessary. I try to be constructive when I critique. I usually succeed.

Ironically, I judged another category in that contest. I hope my entrants receive my critique with the spirit it was given. I want to build people up, not tear them apart. Why rain on somebody's writing parade? I sincerely hope I have judges who judge like me: with kindness in their intent.

On the way home from the workshop, my writing friend and I chatted about what we had learned. We had a four-hour drive so we chatted a lot. We clarified her plot points (Larry Brooks' book continues to help me understand plot and I wish I had read it BEFORE I wrote this MS).

But mine? Hmm, not so much. I did decide that I am not writing a thriller or RS (Romantic Suspense—why are nearly all the examples for writing taken from thrillers and suspense movies?) and that the main conflict is, as always, Boy Meets Girl, Boy and Girl Want Each Other, Boy and Girl Can't Have Each Other, Boy and Girl Find a Way to Be Together. The End. All the other plot stuff is just that—plot stuff. Romance readers want to be entertained, and they want a credible plot, but most of all they want to fall in love with our hero and they want our heroine to deserve him. They want the love to be compelling.

Romance is more about characters than it is about plot.

So here I sit, at my computer with a lot of questions. I also sit here with a lot of ideas and a lot of information. I sit here and wait for contest results to come back so I can digest them and think some more.

Repeat after me: writing doesn't always mean writing words and counting them. Writing takes a lot of thinking, daydreaming, wondering and mulling.

Today I will do a bit more wondering and mulling. I've also decided to talk to my hero and heroine. I'm going to sit down with my Main Characters and ask them a lot of questions. Why? I've realized that I've played Goddess of their lives too many times, and it isn't working for me. I've tried to direct their lives with plots and schemes and ideas. And they aren't cooperating. Therefore I will step aside and let them take charge. I need them to tell me why I should write their story.

Stay tuned. I'll let you know if they reveal their story to me later.

(*May 2015 Note: They did. And I loved it.*)

Writing Isn't Always "Writing"

April 26, 2010

I've reached a point in my revision where I must stop and let my characters reveal the story to me before I jump into the next revision.

Confession: Patience is not one of my higher virtues. I must be forced by circumstances to be patient.

The circumstances I face are:

A. Guests coming in for a week. I am very excited about the family visit. I can't wait to see my brother, my sister-in-law and my niece. We have a lot of fun things planned. This is their first visit to the Southeast. I want to make it a memorable one. This also means not writing a lot.

B. Battling the Veterans Administration again regarding my father-in-law's insurance claims. That's phone calls and waiting and phone calls and waiting and ... lots of time finding the right person to help us help my father-in-law. He's dying of cancer, his wife is focused on him, and we are fighting for his rights. That's called real life. Sometimes real life has to come first.

C. Waiting for responses from my CPs regarding my story sketch. I spent a great deal of time interviewing my characters. My heroine has come out and I know her story. Other characters have revealed themselves. I've got oodles written in backstory regarding the history of why my heroine is where she is and why she wants to stay. I know her inside and out. My hero? Oh, he's being cagey. There's a hole because I had to eliminate so many elements of his backstory to even out the tone of the story. That leaves me questioning why he's back home—it's not just to stop his mom from making, in his mind, a monumental mistake. But he's not fessing up. That means going to the Villain and asking him. I need to interview him and see what he knows.

D. Researching and brainstorming ideas in general. Looking up information about the laws in my state regarding the subject matter. This takes time.

So writing is not always about getting the story revised. Writing is about breaking down the elements and thinking/muddling/talking about the story. I've sat down in front of the computer three times now. I've written a first draft and two revisions. I've entered contests and received feedback regarding the storyline and the characters.

I've been critiqued by a published author and learned more about why my middle is sagging at a workshop. All of these elements, the lessons I've learned, the positive and constructive feedback I've received are gelling in my mind and forcing me to seriously evaluate where the story is going before I sit down to revise it again.

The only problem with this stage of the revision is that inspiration strikes at odd times. I'm not always focused on the real world tasks because one of my characters pipes up and prods me with their information. I have to write this information down quickly or I might lose it. I'm living in two worlds: my fictional world and my real world. They collide on occasion.

The good news is I believe this dual life is helping me shake out the story elements. I'm not feeling pressured to know all the answers this week. I just want to let the characters reveal themselves to me while I clean the kitty litter, shop for groceries for my company, do laundry, exercise, set up the guest room and make my phone calls.

This is all good. I am glad I am forced to be patient. I'll be released to write soon enough.

Keep It Simple Silly

May 3, 2010

Before I head into the ring again to wrestle my WIP in revision into shape, I had to have a meeting with myself to determine just how nuts I'd go with my wrestling technique. I've been banging this WIP's plot hard, punching holes into the plot, taping wounds in the words and sending out 911 distress calls for medical intervention via contests, workshops, brainstorming, and CP/beta reader feedback.

The WIP lies on the desk, a pile of two hundred and fifty printed out pages in a crooked, yet ordered 1-250, jumble. On top of it I've stacked the current short story sketch, two newspapers with articles about tornadoes, contest feedback with useful and constructive criticism and the original GMC (Goal, Motivation, & Conflict) charts I planned a year ago.

In front of me, on the wall above my laptop and desk, are about a dozen Post-it notes with little jottings about the book. They include tidbits about ongoing word counts, reminders about what I want to read and do for my writing, a workshop class list that I am moderating, a few agencies I plan to query, and my RWA® (Romance Writers of America®) membership number. I also have another workshop's lessons about achieving believable romantic resolution taped to the wall.

Surrounding my desk, on the walls and door of my closet and in my bookshelves are my 3rd Revision's story poster board with notes on it in ball point to show the new changes I plan to implement, other craft books, mounds of paper ready for the printer and my collage that I created while brainstorming the first draft of this book (over a year ago!).

In my computer, under the book's title, I have a bunch of files containing all the drafts in my word processor and Scrivener©. I have my contest results (the ones that are helpful), my CP's comments, and my character interviews.

Sigh. The visual clutter is making my mind rebel.

Here are the results of the meeting with myself:

1. I'm not ready to straighten out this mess within my mind. Oh, I've got dozens of ideas and my story is semi plotted again. But I'm not ready to plow into the pile of papers on my desk and make it all work.

2. I will be ready to straighten out this mess by the end of the week. My butt is in the fire. I entered the MAGGIE with this story. I have to find a way to carve out 30 decent pages of writing and a new synopsis reflecting my

story's evolving plot. I've got to do it by June 1.

3. I've determined that this is my final lob of the revision ball. After I enter the MAGGIE with what I put together, I will focus and keep on revising until the end of June.

4. During the first part of July, I'm pulling together my pitch for Nationals and the Moonlight & Magnolias Conference®.

5. But will I continue to revise this book after July 1? Yes, but only after I get a request. If I don't get a request, what is the point? I need to take what I've learned and apply it to the next book.

6. It's time to Keep It Simple Silly. It's time to focus on what I can fix, not worry about rewriting the entire plot again, and toss the book out there to see if there is any interest in it by people who will represent me or pay me to fix it.

If I stay mired in this book, I'll be writing four books and only have one to show for it. Not going to work. Not anymore. I've got to finish it to the best of my ability, but I don't have to keep reinventing the wheel. This summer I need to move on so I can write the book that might be the one that gets my foot in the door.

I'm keeping it simple so I can free myself for the next idea and the next book.

You've Got to Play to Work

October 22, 2010

Last week I posted about finding your dream and going for it with no excuses. My first tip to pursuing one's dreams and goals was to make time to do it. There is no such thing as no time to do anything unless you are working three jobs and raising a family. There just isn't. If you have a half an hour, you've got time to work toward your goal.

Establishing a minimum time requirement per day is crucial toward reaching your goal. Even if all you do is research what it will take to accomplish reaching your goal, then it is still productive use of your time. As a writer, that half an hour might be about researching some facet of my novel. But if you're dreaming about becoming a doctor, it might be about researching what areas of medicine are best suited to your personality. Each step, even a baby step, is still a step forward.

I haven't been working as much as I've been playing. In fact, I didn't even meet one of my big goals for the week because I preferred playing to sitting down and reading through my two requested partial manuscripts. I always like to do a read-aloud before I do my final tweak and send my babies out into the world.

Bad me! But not really. Why? I managed to meet my minimum goals every day this week. I also exceeded them more days than not. My minimum goal this week was to write 100 words a day about my new book which I am exploring, follow up on blog comments, write three blogs for the following week and schedule them, continue working on my social media knowledge via Kristen Lamb's book *We Are Not Alone* and my online courses. Yes, despite my deliberate hooky from serious work, I managed to accomplish quite a lot.

I could have accomplished more if I had hunkered down and forced myself to stop playing and work. But I know something important: my brain needs a break and this season is the one season I feel fully rejuvenated if I take the time to play. Every year in the autumn I slow down a bit to let my brain relax and enjoy the beautiful season.

Usually I've been working super hard and this year was no exception. I was working on my full manuscript's revision until September 29. On September 30, I immediately went to the Georgia Writers of America® Moonlight and Magnolia's Conference® and immersed myself in all things professional via pitching my manuscript, learning about writing from Michael Hauge, Allison Brennan and Kelly Stone, and celebrating my writing friends' victories at the MAGGIE Awards Ceremony.

There wasn't much time to breathe between that trip and our fall break with the family. I knew it would be pointless to undertake a large project so I stuck to my mini goals and gave myself some space.

This is my second tip: Understand your rhythm as you undertake pursuing your goal.

If you don't understand how you work and when it is best for you to work, then you will burn out. Everyone has a different rhythm. I tend to operate well on long jags of intense work with time out for good behavior breaks. I need my social time, my sun time and my time to relax if I am going to get the big tasks done. I've also learned that as a writer, I must touch or do something with my current work in progress everyday or I'll lose my connection with my story. Now that doesn't mean I write through major holidays like Christmas or New Years Eve, but I do write a bit every day through almost all the days of the year.

The trick is I know when to notch back my efforts and I don't beat myself up for not attaining major goals. I can make up for the loss during high workdays. Giving myself permission to chill helps me to work harder when I am on full schedule. This can be true of students. I used to look at my schedules and I could see where my days were filled and not so filled. I made sure I cut back a bit, let myself play and regroup, during those slower days.

It's important to know when you're strongest creatively. Is it mornings? Nights? Afternoons? I tend to be super awake and creative in the mornings, lull in the afternoons, and then pick up a bit again in the 4PM-6PM time slot. Afternoon lulls are when I usually play more during my "off time" but if I am in full work zone, I usually use afternoons to catch up on the business and boring parts of my job as a writer.

Years ago I read a great book by Dr. Robert Arnot called *The Biology of Success*. I still have it in my bookshelf and refer to it regularly. Understand how you operate and you will optimize your chances of succeeding in your chosen profession.

Flexible Writing (Yoga Optional)

March 3, 2011

I once met a mother who said she liked me because I was a "flexible" parent. No. I can't do the splits or turn a cartwheel, but I have learned that sometimes rolling with the child's schedule and adjusting the parenting dial of discipline helps me be a better mother.

I wish I could say I am always in tune and know when to adjust the dial, but I am not perfect. Sometimes I just realize that there are too many bumps in the parenting road and I rethink my position about how to handle my attempts to raise a well-rounded citizen of the world.

The same can be said about my writing. I'm a writer. I write stories. I have goals and personal deadlines because I treat my writing like a job, not a hobby. I am a professional, unpaid writer who desires publication. I tend to move forward in a nice, linear fashion when I start my books. I write fast. Messy, sloppy first drafts are my game. I like to get the story out.

It doesn't seem to matter how much I plan, the map is not even a guideline by the time I get to the middle of the book. Things get quite murky and I toss the dang outline aside just to keep writing forward. I've learned I'm better at tearing apart a first draft and finding the real story inside the shell I've created so I'm always itchy to finish my first draft. That's when the real writing can begin.

This year I set my writing goals. One goal was to complete two books in a four book series. I outlined four books. I had my characters all planned out. I had the story arc for the entire series written out in an overview. I had the first book plotted/outlined and I began writing it in earnest in January. It's finished, but not really, because I had another project pop into my life that required my setting aside the book I was working on, rethinking the entire series in a new way, and working on a revision for another book.

I had to do the *downward facing dog* of writing yoga and look at everything from a different perspective. I had to be flexible as a writer. Twist my brain inside out and make it work in a new way. The only thing I knew I was capable of doing was the cutting of the debris that was no longer deemed necessary. But once I cut the debris out, would I have a story? Would the characters I had not hung out with for a long while actually come out to play again? I immediately went into "child's pose" and whimpered a bit at the prospect.

Even worse, I had to wait to start. I am not a patient sort, so waiting was very hard. Very very very very very hard. I admit it: I am not good at biding my time. I was actually quite worried about the waiting period. The dominoes of time were falling fast. I panicked. I was very scared I'd fail before I started. I'd lost so much time (my freakish obsession with time is legendary in my family—I'm not allowed to wear a watch when we go on vacation as a result). Thankfully, I have amazing friends and writing partners who encouraged me and told me I had plenty of time. The dominoes slowly reassembled into their neat little timelines during my biding time.

Waiting was actually a good thing. It gave me time to think, mull, ask questions, search my mind for solutions, and cajole my characters out of my noggin. Biding my time meant I could gently tiptoe back into the story while banging out the first draft of the other story I was writing. When I finally sat down to work on the revision, I had a more flexible attitude about the entire process.

Now that I am in revision mode, I've also realized that the type of writing I do often impacts where I sit down to write. I can write a first draft anywhere, any time, any amount of words. There are no constrictions to the writing. It flows. I can tune out the people and noises so easily when I am in first draft mode. I can write in airports, restaurants, coffee shops. I just write.

Revisions? Not so easy. I have to literally move my computer out of the office and sit at another table so I'm not tempted to do the business of writing—okay, check emails and Facebook and tweet. I readily confess that I am great at distracting myself in the cyber world. During revisions, I need to sit at a table, in the kitchen area, with my notebook close at hand. I have to think more, jot notes, walk away, come back, sit down, pour tea, anything I can do to trick my characters into telling me more about their story.

It is their story. I know their story. I have it inside me. I'm slowly letting it come out and trying really hard to be patient with my characters. Whenever my patience is tried, I get up and walk away. I adjust my thinking. I return with a new idea and ask them, "Is this what you were trying to tell me two years ago? Oh, okay, I get it. Then I will write it for you."

I also take a lot of showers. No matter what kind of writing phase I am in, I tend to get the greatest inspiration while washing my hair and putting on my makeup.

The Dark Night of the Soul: All is Lost

April 6, 2011

I'm a writer. I write commercial fiction. I follow a basic structure and format as I cobble together my story. I also let the muse come in and dance when I am in first draft mode. This dance releases me from the handcuffs of perfection. However, it does not release me from the reality of following a basic map. I need a guideline of sorts that gives me an idea of where I'm supposed to end up. Every story, whether carefully plotted or not, must have certain elements in it in order to fly into the publishing world.

Some of the elements are compelling characters, a unique hook or high concept, an interesting plot line, and a mastery of basic writing craft. I'll be the first to admit that grammar is my least favorite element to master. I'm a decent writer, an intuitive writer, but I am not a super technical writer. I don't have years of technical writing as a profession, nor do I have a degree in English, Literature, or journalism. But I don't believe I need any of those things in my background to be a good, compelling storyteller.

That's what I am and what I have always been. A storyteller. An imaginative, creative, daydreamer with thousands of ideas and wonderings about how people mesh together despite the odds against them. I'd like to believe that I have a lot to give as a writer because I also have a wealth of experience that comes from having lived a life that wasn't perfect. I've experienced loss, loneliness, extreme fear, the daunting aspect of where will I live tomorrow? I've experienced hunger, real hunger. I didn't have enough money to pay both the rent and the grocery bill. I've experienced the Dark Night of the Soul. I know what is like to believe All Is Lost.

Understanding the Dark Night of the Soul is a key element to writing compelling stories. If I had always had everything run smoothly in my life and if I always received accolades for my hard work, I'd never be able to truly translate the dark night of the soul onto the page.

What is the dark night of the soul in the writing world? In novels it is the part of the book where the reader believes the hero and or heroine have lost everything. There's been a terrible black moment. In a romance, the black moment is emotionally gripping. The hero and heroine walk away from each other because they believe they've lost their chance at true love. They believe all is lost and there is no way back. But they're wrong. As a writer, I owe it to my readers to bring these two people back together. They do deserve each other. How they've grown emotionally, despite their backgrounds and their emotional baggage constantly driving them apart, is the way they will find a path to each other.

The dark night of the soul is an intensely personal, emotional moment for the hero and the heroine. As much as I'd like to make my readers laugh a little, the truth is that at this moment if my readers aren't reaching for a tissue, I've failed. This isn't easy stuff to write, folks. This is mining the heart. This is where the technically sound, pulled together neat little story might just fall apart. Why? The depth of emotion isn't there for the reader. They aren't sad. They aren't feeling anything. They may even think the couple should stay apart.

In fiction, the Dark Night of the Soul is resolved by the writer's words. In real life, the Dark Night of the Soul isn't so easily resolved. So how do we mere humans, myself included, survive and grow past the feeling that All is Lost? We can't rewrite the terrible circumstances. We can't re-order the world into a nice, neat box. We can't make the pain of the loss evaporate in an instant.

I think if we allow ourselves to feel the pain, to know the pain, to acknowledge the pain then we will get through it because we've been honest with ourselves about our emotions. We need to reach out to our most trusted friends and life's companions and reveal the truth about the darkness within. Even C.S. Lewis suffered from extreme bouts of depression. He turned to his friends for guidance, for support, for encouragement.

I experienced the Dark Night of the Soul when I was sixteen years old. I could no longer live at home, but I had no place to go. I had no relatives to take me in. I had no one to watch over me. I was as alone as a girl can be with my one blue suitcase in my hand. That was all I possessed: one suitcase of clothing. I literally had no place to go. But a girl I'd barely known, someone I'd briefly shared my sad tale with while at school, had told her mother about me and this family of strangers took me in. They housed me for over a year.

I've experienced the Dark Night of the Soul. I remember calling my best friend up when I thought I could never have a child. I was ironing (I always iron when I am scared or upset). I'd suffered so many miscarriages that this last pregnancy attempt was literally my last go. I just couldn't face another loss. I needed her to hear my pain, to hear me cry and wail at the wall of my misery of loss. I needed to unleash the firestorm of anger, sorrow, and agony within me because I was going to be denied the one thing I so desperately wanted. She said she'd carry a baby for me if I needed her. That was when the darkness lifted. I wasn't alone.

I've experienced the Dark Night of the Soul. I remember working on my third manuscript when I received a call from my best friend's husband. He was unusually calm, yet he wasn't himself. My friend had a diseased kidney that had to be removed. They were 99% sure she had cancer. The sheer drop of my heart into my stomach can't even begin to describe my fear for her. For me. This woman who had known me through many of my dark nights, who'd held my child and cared for her when I was finally blessed with a baby, who'd counseled me wisely and without holding back, was in danger.

There wasn't a thing I could do to stop it.

For three weeks we waited for news about her life. Three. Long. Weeks. We talked a lot. We laughed a lot. But behind the laughter there was a beast of dread so dark in the pit of my stomach that I couldn't focus, couldn't breath, couldn't relax. What if all was lost? I turned to my faith, my friends, and my hope for encouragement. The day my friend called to say she was cancer free ranks up there in the top 5 golden moments of my life. The house rang with our joy, it bounced off the ceiling and ping ponged around the rooms as we laughed our first unrestrained laughs in weeks.

The Dark Night of the Soul. All is Lost. But nothing is lost until we give up and say there is no hope. That is what we as writers, as people, must strive for in our lives. Cultivate hope. Cultivate friendships that nurture your hope. Hope restores light into our lives, into our characters' lives, and restores us to a place of peace and happiness.

Crossroads, Forks and Detours: Goals Reevaluated

May 23, 2011

I'm approaching another end of a quarter and am reevaluating my priorities. I do so every 3 months. I've decided to work up a mini-fix for the month of June because this quarter has been a wild one. I'm only 2 months into the quarter and it feels like it has lasted 6 months! I must step back and regroup so I can strengthen my focus. Basically, I'm de-cluttering my mind of useless stuff so I can tackle the important events coming up this month.

This quarter I started strong with an R & R (Revise and Resubmit) out the door and the rest of the story to revise. It's been about two months since I sent the R & R out and I am in "wait mode." So much of this business is about waiting and being patient, but while writers wait we must do only one thing: write some more. So I finished the rest of the revision, sent it off to my CP, and tackled her critique three chapters at a time. I have three more chapters to go and I'm finished this round. That's on the table for the first part of this week.

While I revised this book, I entered another contest (which still requires an entry), learned I finaled in the Fab Five writing contest, and attended a great workshop. I returned home in mid-April ready to work my tail off. Then the first detour in my road occurred. Sick kid. Mono. She's been home for about a month and a half now. I've got to admit, it's put a cramp in my writing style. You see, I am a bit spoiled. She's a teenager who drives so I was used to the days being mine to do my work. I had to work around her doctor appointments, caring for her, organizing school work, and canceling a lot of her "life" until she got better.

But as Nora Roberts says, glass balls are more important than rubber ones. My daughter's health, my daughter period, is glass. Fragile, precious glass I cherish. Writing will always come second to my child. Always. She needed me. I was there for her. I still am. I managed to revise a bit more, but a week after my child's diagnosis, the skies opened up and all hell broke loose in Alabama. We experienced 28 tornadoes in 1 day. The most terrifying day ever. I don't think I'll ever forget the sirens, the dark skies, the sudden pop above my head after an eerie silence, or the complete sense of helplessness.

We were lucky. We didn't suffer any damage or injuries and I'm so grateful. But my writing did suffer a setback. Not just because of the time lost, but because my heart was aching. I was sore. Sad. I just wanted to reconnect with my friends. Talk.

Sleep. Be still. Pray. I did. I gave myself permission to take a bit of a break.

I took a look at the crossroad in front of me and went left instead of right. I enjoyed the journey. I played with a new story idea, came up with plot points, index cards, and just had fun. I ignored the revision for a bit. That was great. I reevaluated my future writing projects. I relaxed. Well, I relaxed for me. Anyone who knows me knows I am not a "relaxed" kind of gal. In the midst of all of this there was still the sick kid, still the doctor visits, still the desire to create, still the household to keep up, still the new diet to cook dozens of meals for......... and so the relaxation was more of a pit stop here and there punctuated with bursts of work.

Of course, part of my idea of relaxing was to take a break from revisions and plan a new story. In the midst of story boarding my next novel, I managed to snag a couple of great editor and agent appointments at the RWA® National Conference®. Usually Nationals are in July, but this year the conference is June 28-July 2. I have very little time to prepare for it because of, oh, the above paragraphs. But that's okay. I can pull it off. I plan on pulling this off after I finish the first draft of my next book, and after I tour two more colleges with my darling teen (who is slowly mending despite another minor health setback).

Life is happening. All. The. Time. Somehow writers must continue to write despite the many distractions. The only way I know how to do that is to have a plan. A map. Of course, the map can't prepare us for every detour and crossroad that comes our way, but it can give us a place to refer to when we get a little lost. Sometimes a new map needs to take the place of the old map.

Think You've Got No Time?
Think Again

November 14, 2011

I can't tell you how many times I've heard someone say, "I'd write a book if only I had the time."

Hmmm. No time? Let me tell you something. If you have thirty minutes a day then you have time. What? You don't have thirty minutes? You're super busy? Hmmmmmmmmmm.... I bet you have a half an hour of time that is just wasted.

Think about it. Do you really use every minute of your day productively? Write down every meaningless task you do and how often you do it and for how long. Dillydallying on the computer? Internet Squirrels to chase? Answering emails first? Volunteering your time versus using your time to write? Answering the phone even if it isn't an emergency?

Okay, here's my story. A lot of people ask me how I do it all and keep it straight. My first answer is "I don't do it all." Check my bathrooms out as well as my floors. House is not spotless and it never will be spotless. I also don't work in what we writers call a DDJ (Dreaded Day Job). Lots of published authors work DDJs or DNJ's (Dreaded Night Job) and they have deadlines to meet. So not using my time during the day wisely is just wrong.

Oh, I could use it differently. I could have an immaculate house. I could have tons of social activities during the day to attend. I could volunteer ALL my hours away. I could shop and decorate on a dime. I could have other hobbies. I... well... I don't do it all. If I want to be a career writer, then I have to prioritize. So a perfect house which is perfectly decorated and pursuing all sorts of hobbies just aren't on my agenda.

Housework? I ask for help and if I don't get it, then the house goes to Defcon 102 and we all have to pitch in to clean. No one in my house likes it to get too dirty. Social life? Here I have virtually none—which is a problem because I am very social, but I digress. Here's the deal. I like to spend time with people who don't write, too. So I make sure that my evenings are clear. I don't write as much on the weekends, but then I don't have a pesky DDJ/DDN so I am lucky.

Here's another secret. I am scandalously unmoved by the ringing phone. Yes, it's true. I don't answer the phone. This is my biggest defense against time sucks. Don't answer the phone unless it is the school, the hospital, the doctor. Not for anyone during your allotted writing time (*May 2015 Note: If my daughter calls, I answer—her calls are always important to me.*) This includes calls from neighbors who are wondering where you are or friends who want to gab and gab and gab. This doesn't mean that I never talk on the phone. I just plan my phone time around my writing schedule.

I don't answer the phone during my writing time unless it is my daughter calling, her school, or the Physicist. They are the important people. The Physicist is often sent to voice mail and then I check it during my break (yup—my break) and see if it is important. Same goes for friends—unless it's a friend in another country. I will answer due to the time difference. But usually I just let the answering machine pick it up—in my case it's voice mail and I have a phone voice announce out loud who is calling so I know when to let it go to voice mail. I don't even have to get out of my chair to check the caller ID.

Cool right?

I volunteer, but very sporadically. I help with my daughter's theater group and do some things with my local writing chapters. But I have even backed off the writing volunteer stuff because my daughter is graduating in 2012 and I want to have time with her. Plus senior year is just insane and there are a lot of holes to plug before the big graduation day.

Time is precious. I spend time with people who are precious to me. So here's another secret: I don't let things like other people's expectations or the phone or the Internet own me. I am in charge of those things. I own my response. I own my time. I own my writing time.

Your writing time: Own it or you will have blown it.

Okay. Want one more secret? Use downtime productively. For instance, today I had to color my hair (I don't go to the salon unless I'm getting a cut or highlights or both. And that's rare these days). Roots were rearing and I needed to get my blonde going on before I forced my minions, AKA my daughter and the Physicist, to help me clean this behemoth of a house. There's no point in sparkling up the bathroom if I throw dye down the sink.

So what's a girl to do while she waits for her blonde to set? Thirty minutes is a long time. Here's what I did while my hair cooked to it's "natural" blonde again.

- Tidied up the living room.
- Cleaned the guest bathroom (company coming tonight for dinner).
- Cleaned the kitty litter (must talk to the minions about this—not my turn but it smelled bad).
- Loaded the dishwasher.
- Checked my voicemail.
- Called the Physicist to ask for info for the school.
- Called the school and gave the person info asked for in the voicemail.
- Emptied the garbage.
- Played with my kitten Tonks.
- Wiped out my sink so Tonks wouldn't lick errant hair dye particles.

That's what I accomplished during the time my hair was becoming blonde again. Thirty minutes is a lot of time. You can write half a page in thirty minutes. You can work on getting the synopsis for your story ready for thirty minutes.

What Happens Next? Why does it Matter? Lessons to Think About

December 16, 2011

I live in a fictional world where the main question is often *What happens next?* What are the characters doing, where are they doing it, and why are they doing it and does what they are doing matter to them and to the story?

What happens next? Sometimes I don't know. Sometimes I think I know. Sometimes I fool myself about knowing which leads to many revisions. I believe this is because I haven't sat down with my characters and discussed why they are doing what they are doing next. What drives the characters drives the story forward.

More than anything in the past year I have learned that if I play Goddess of My Manuscript, my characters rebel. This means slowing down, looking at what I've written and asking "is this really what they are doing next?" How do I know for sure? I don't. I just have to write it out, mull it over, look at it again, and play with the story until the manuscript gels.

Even then I know that someone will come along and poke holes into what I believe has been the solution all along. First, it will be critique partners. Second, it will be contest judges. Third, it will be editors and agents. I know I will have to write again. And again and again.

But I do know one thing—I must first write the story as I see it unfold from beginning to end before I make monumental changes to it. I must first revise it at least once before I start sending it out to my critique partners. I need to discover my story before I let other people tell me what the story should be about and mess up my relationship with my characters.

Oh, I can brainstorm. I can call up a CP and tell them I have an idea about a scene in the current WIP and what do you think? They might agree or disagree, but it's called bouncing ideas off someone to see if the ideas can work. There's no point in writing something if it won't work.

I have to be in my characters' heads. I have to think with their thoughts. I have to react as they would react. And I have to do all of this on blank pages by filling them with words. Words I have written to the best of my ability.

So here are my basic rules for writing:

1. Write the first draft for you and the characters. Don't let anyone TOUCH your

story or critique it without knowing it well enough.

2. Brainstorming is a good thing. Bounce ideas off people to see if they will gel with the story regardless of where you are in the process. They'll either be affirmed or not. But ultimately, it is your story so you must decide how to fix it in the end.

3. Be prepared to make changes after you have completed your manuscript.

4. Even when you think you're finished—even if you are published and have an editor—be prepared to make more changes.

5. In romances, characters trump everything. Write them well and make them jump off the page and you will get interest in your work. And then guess what?

6. Be prepared to make changes to your characters based on editorial and agent input.

7. Stay with your story and think about it every day so you can be open to the revelations your characters send you when you are in the shower, in the bath, driving long distances, sitting through boring meetings, putting on makeup, cleaning floors. Trust me. If you stay with your story every day, you will find ideas popping into your head at odd times.

8. Judges comments are to be taken with a grain of salt. They are not the final word. They can be wrong. They can be right. But ultimately, the reason you enter a contest is

to get to the final judge—an editor or an agent. I personally have incorporated good comments and suggestions into my writing, but never until I give it thought and time.

9. Editors and agents send revise and resubmit letters. It is up to you to decide if they are right about their suggestions. If you decide to Revise and Resubmit, You don't have to do everything they say either. They are giving you suggestions based on their instinct and knowledge. But ultimately it is up to your characters to drive the story.

10. Trust your instincts. Trust yourself. Trust your characters.

Refueling Before Revisions: My Writing Process

March 2, 2012

I've discovered a lot about my writing process since I began this journey. I believe I am Crapper Pantser Plotter Fixer Upper writer.

In other words: Messy but as many critique partners have attested, I *clean up well.* Here's how it usually rolls for me:

1. I get an idea about a story. Usually it's spurred by a show, or a news item, or some weird bizarre trip of a neuron wire inside my brain. I have more ideas than I know what to do with and some of them are kind of not going to work with the current line I'm targeting. But I always keep them and I have files everywhere, notebooks everywhere, you name it.

2. The characters. I have a distinct scene in my head where the hero/heroine meet. How they

meet. What's in their heads. What I don't have is their profession, their looks, their names. I just have a scene with dialogue and thought and bodies moving around a vacuous space. Sometimes there is more. But usually they're just talking and I see them moving around, little nuances and gestures and tones of voice are often revealed.

(*May 2015 Note: Ever since I started working with my critique partner, Pam Mantovani, I have made it a point to have first, middle, and last names in place before I write.*)

3. The idea grows into a blurb, which I mold into a logline—the logline/tagline may not be pretty, but it's mine and I own it.

4. I brainstorm with friends, critique partners, myself to flesh out the characters' reason for being together, who they are and what they look like, what the story will be about and the basic turning points I know I have to reach. I lay down my tent poles/get the bones of the story ready.

5. I write a synopsis based on the first four steps. Truthfully, I just did for the first time before I had the story written in discovery phase with the current WIP. The trick is to let go of what you originally thought was going to happen and revamp it as you go along. The current synopsis does not match the original synopsis, but it's been easy to

fix the original. Way easier than writing one after the manuscript is completed.

6. I write a quick discovery draft, flesh out the bones a bit,

7. I really work on the first three chapters and polish them because they are part of the partial/proposal I need to query.

8. I retool the story based on critique, suggestions, my characters telling me I'm going in the wrong direction.

9. I go in to add meat, and to take away some of the original flesh of the rest of the story based on what I'm discovering about the characters and about their love story. I do this fast, but as grammatically correct as possible (don't ask me about the commas). By this point I've cut a lot and I've added a lot.

10. I let the first revision sit for a few days while I listen to craft tapes, read other books in my genre, mull my ideas and my story, catch up on the business side of the writing world (my least favorite part but it has to be done), query, print out my book and let it sit around the office (or the tornado shelter), catch up on household mundaneness and with friends who wondered where I was for a few weeks.

11. I begin revising in batches. I send the revised batches, usually 3 chapters at a time, to CPs and continue revising forward. I don't utilize the critique until I am ready for another round of revisions.

12. I export everything to Word and work with the complete document, formatting and cleaning up Scrivener© burps. I'm not that technical so I tend to have a lot of driver error in this export stuff. But I think it just forces me to look at the book in a new way, which is a good thing.

13. I continue polishing and shining up the story. I layer in more visceral elements and look for things like sensory items I can add to the story. But I don't overwork it. I would drive myself insane if I did that, so I begin working on the next book. Pre-writing.

14. I start entering contests with the newest manuscript. I move forward on the next book. I query. I go through it all over again.

My goal is to get faster at this gig. I must generate 3-4 category series romances per year to be a successful career writer and build readership. I'm glad I have a "future list" ready to go out the door, but I want to write more. Three to four 48,000-50,000 word (180-190 page count) books means getting one done every three to four months for the editor.

For me this currently means getting faster at revising during the meat phase. I already had the 1st three chapters polished and critiqued and much of the legwork done. The ending always echoes the beginning for me and I can usually visualize the scenes very clearly. I know the black moment and how they will resolve it to a point. I just keep layering in new stuff and getting rid of stuff that doesn't work. But I don't have beautiful prose until at least the 3rd time through. I still have work to do. This isn't easy for me. I work hard. Really hard. With this current WIP, I want to deliver on the first three chapters' promise. So I am determined to write it fast, write it smart, and be focused during this month despite the fact that I have a lot of travel interrupting my time.

This means I cut a lot of words. But I like cutting. I like revising. I am the Queen of Revision. I know of no other way to allow the actual story to unfold than by getting rid of beloved words and scenes and people. Oh, I keep them all in another file, but the story demands I make changes. This is a good mindset to get into as I have had a Revise and Resubmit letter from editors at a publishing house. Basically, I had to cut 30 thousand words and start all over again to take the story in a new direction with the same characters. They even asked me to change THE PREMISE. So I did. We'll see how the new premise flies.

Right now I am in Stage 10 and getting ready for Stage 11. I am printing out my batches today. Fritzing around with the business of writing stuff, and giving my wee brain a break.

Reality Check: The Book Comes First

June 18, 2012

I've been in La La Land for over ten days. First a trip to Los Angeles, which was interesting, different, fun, wild, weird, and wacky. Then the piles of laundry and cleaning and readjusting to life back in Alabama. Finally, the Darling Teen had her five wisdom teeth pulled last Friday and she's been recuperating for three days. I'm Mother Henning her to bits but this is my last chance to "baby" her before she heads off to university in August (I was a child bride and had her before I turned twenty—really *grin*). The schedule has been out of whack for days and I need to wrap my brain around another round of revisions.

What falls by the wayside first? Well, besides cleaning commodes that is... social media. Yes, I'm 'supposed' to blog, tweet, post Facebook status updates, learn more about how to utilize Goodreads as an author, and try to figure out if Pinterest is a viable Social Media outlet to use.

But—and this is a big but—I have nothing to promote if I don't have a book written and on sale. Period. The end. I often think that newbie writers—even PRO RWA® (PRO is a status attained within the RWA® that emphasizes the completion of a novel or novella) writers who aren't published—spend far too much time figuring out their brand and their social media outlets and web pages rather than writing. Let's face it, it's easier to play on Twitter and fool around with web pages than revising. Heck, I'm guilty of playing hours of mindless Spider Solitaire while I was en route during my vacation rather than attempting to write. Of course, I knew revising while on a family vacation was not going to happen easily. So I surrendered to that reality and focused on what I had to focus on: the family. I brainstormed, but I didn't do much else.

I don't usually take a big break from writing—haven't for years—but circumstances forced the break and it was useful in that it helped me clarify what to focus on when I sit down to revise this current book. This isn't a do or die revision. It's part of the process that I hope I will become much faster at accomplishing once I'm under contract. I do expect that to become a new reality for me in the near future. I have to expect it. I have to want it. I have to need it. I am hungry for it.

I plan to make a meal out of my writing. A continuous buffet of writing.

Curiously, this all brings me around to the social media versus writing a book soapbox. I can't write and revise if my brain is all wrapped up in technical goop. It requires a different set of brain cells and drains my creativity. So here are my quick and dirty rules for managing social media and not letting it manage you.

1. The book trumps everything. First write, then tweet.

2. If you love to tweet on Twitter, then utilize the #1k1hr hash tag. Look for other writers to write with for an hour, then post your accomplishments on the hour, Tweet something personal to someone in a conversation, Retweet someone's promo tweet. Then back to #1k1hr

3. Twitter not your world? Facebook is your thing? Then post on the hour or 3 times a day or only in the times when your brain is a wet noodle and all you can do is write status updates.

4. Want to build a web page? Don't unless you're close to achieving publication. A blog on Wordpress© or Blogger© will suffice until you get closer. How you go about building it is up to you. I've chosen to go the do it yourself route for now with GoDaddy.com. My Teen can help with the web design fast pages while I *ahem* write my books.

5. Interested in Goodreads or Pinterest, but not sure which route to go? I suggest Goodreads because that is where the readers are located.

6. Blog regularly if you are a new writer to help hone your voice. Blog irregularly the closer you get to the call. You can't blog and write great fiction at the same time. The book trumps the blog. Always.

   (May 2015 Note: I rarely blog now that I am published. There isn't enough time to do it all.)

7. Emailing, Yahoo Groups and more. Email twice a day. No more. Shut down all email programs when you are writing. Turn them off!! Don't see how many emails are in your in-box and be tempted to turn away from that tricky writing problem to email someone back. Yahoo Groups: do digest. Check it once a day. Don't go crazy and try to keep up with all of it. Flag important emails and messages and cope with them when you are ready to cope with them. Online classes? I use digest only mode and print out the lessons to read later. Developing a workshop, or promoting one? Great. Is your book finished? There's no point in getting your name out there if you haven't got a book to sell. The book and your name are your brand.

8. Real face time beats Facebook time. Get out into the world a bit more. Be kind to people you deal with whether it is in the grocery store checkout line, at the gym during a workout class, or as part of a neighborhood community or book club. I already have a wonderful group of people who know I

write in all of these places. Guess what? They aren't on Twitter or blogging. They are working, working out, reading, playing, being moms and dads and friends and more. Be in the world when you are out in public. Don't hide behind the cell phone screen and post tweets all the time on Tweetdeck. Be REAL. Then real people will become interested in you and what you do and you might just sell them your first book!

9. Family time first, then Internet time, or share it with the family.

10. The book trumps everything that's tied to social media, the Internet, emailing, workshops. The book is the only thing that matters. Put the writing first.

I'm done tooting my horn about social media versus real time and writing time. What's on my agenda for the rest of the week? Revisions, looking after the Teen, working out, being a wife and a friend, and popping into the Internet to say hi to all my virtual friends near and far when I'm on a mini break or during the evening when my brain cells turn to rust and creative writing is wrapped up for the day.

Battling the Demons of Doubt and Despair

Ah Well—Close but No Cigar

February 8, 2009

I got back my contest entry for Linda Howard Award of Excellence®. I got a composite score of 176, almost finaled! Yeah, but the problem is with my hero, and I don't know what to do to fix it. Of course, I am disappointed. But I did get excellent feedback. All 5's on the writing and motivation and the overall craft elements. I also got back an "edited" manuscript, and I am not sure what I am going to do with it. I am so close. But I am not there. Yet.

Oh well. I printed it all out, and popped into the manuscript's box and have emailed my two writing buddies in VA to share with them. I can't really worry about the problems I have to fix with that story. I need to focus on the 4th book and let this one slide away for a bit.

But it is so frustrating. Things I cut because of other contests were asked for in this one. Argh, argh, argh! I am beyond pissed about that. Mostly at myself. This is what I sent to the GH, so now I have no hope at all of even coming close to finaling. Or selling this POS. Maybe the next one. Maybe, maybe, maybe…

And then, talking with the Physicist, he's like *Why are you doing this if you probably won't make more than a few thousand dollars a year??* I don't know how to answer that to him. I love writing. But I do want to make some money. I'd be happy if I made a $1000 a year or something. Hell, I'd be happy if I finally got the *Call*. But that isn't happening any time too soon.

The good news is that the story can be fixed. It does have very strong elements. Someone might buy it. One day. I told myself fifty years old, or bust. I've got four more years to slog away at this. Then I'll have written for ten years. Seven books, ten years before you're published. That is the adage. We'll see where I am at that point.

Meanwhile, maybe I can write a motivational lecture for non-published writers about how to get up and face the computer even if no one else reads your shit but contest judges, other writers, and your friends.

Sigh.

Fighting the Twin Demons of Doubt and Fear

February 9, 2009

I am ready to get rolling on this book in a week. I already have easy to cook stuff in the freezer and my daughter is so wrapped up in school play rehearsals and dance next week, she'll subsist on sandwiches for three of the days. LOL.

I had to fight to get my right brain back in line this week. I got a contest entry result for the third book back via email on Sunday and, though I didn't final, I did score very well and got some good feedback. The bad part about this is it made me want to A) Tinker with the biggest problem both judges saw regarding a first meeting scene between the hero and heroine, and B) All the storyline/characters for the third book came and interfered with this new book. Argh.

Then the whole doubt, fear why am doing this when I have to send a kid to college in three years and I am not financially rewarded for playing with these stories resurfaced. I was definitely blue. I opened the closet door with all my *successes and reasons why I am cut out for this crazy field* and read my favorite quote by Delle Jacobs *"The object of goals is getting there... the object of dreams is the journey."* I felt a bit better after I read it. Then I called a writing buddy and said, look, can you read this for me? Don't give me any feedback until March cause I can't think about this book until then. She agreed to do it. Then I sent it to a good friend who just likes reading my stuff for me, and asked her to do the same.

That helped. I am querying the book to three publishers this week so I can tell the Physicist I am at least trying to sell the dang thing. How does one explain to one's people how bloody hard this industry is???? But I will succeed. I have to

Climbing Mountains

March 9, 2009

I have heard a song on the radio that pretty much says it all. I love the lyrics. It's a great song and it encompasses all I think about when it comes to writing:

There is always another mountain to climb...

No matter where we are in our careers or on this journey, we will always have mountains standing in our way. We will always have boulders in our path blocking our passage, and we will always have rivers to navigate to get to the other side. The trick is doing it. Doing it in spite of the worry, the fear, the doubts, the concerns, and the possibility of failing. The trick is to believe that the mountain can be climbed, the boulder can be moved out of the way, and the river can be navigated safely.

The courage to face the fear and do it anyway is not in all of us. But it is in some of us. Even that courage doesn't mean success. Not outwardly. But it does mean success within. The knowledge of one's fortitude is success. How many times did Rocky get hit? How many times did we fight any enemy nation and think we'd lose? But we did it anyway. We performed.

The trick is to keep working and performing despite the obstacles in our way. The trick is to keep working and performing even when no one comes to watch the show.

That is the hardest lesson to learn. When we have only an audience of one, we still have to perform.

Moving Past a Lovely Rejection

October 14, 2009

Dear Writer—your writing voice is very compelling, but your tone is more like romantic comedy, not a spicy read (if only I could have sent one sex scene say I). Now the beat begins—what to do when the rejection isn't about the writing, but the tone being wrong for the line I specifically targeted?

- First, I call my CPs who encouraged me to zip the puppy out and query it to at least 6 other agents—the writing is strong—let an agent find a home for it. Fish for an agent... okie dokie.
- Second, plan on the GH® submission for said novel. Perhaps if it finals, more interest will be generated in it.
- Third, throw a personal pity party complete with 80s music and red wine.
- Fourth, wake up super early and hit the office hard.

- Fifth, make a plan of action for the next six weeks.
- Sixth, throw off the mantle of disappointment and remind myself that many very successful authors have suitcases full of rejections.
- Seventh, develop a plan to make my blog more exciting (stay tuned).
- Eighth, make time to read a writing friend's MS.
- Ninth, remind myself that I am in the water, the waves will find me and carry me to where I belong with my writing. I am not chasing trends. I must continue to search for the elusive, *something more.*
- Tenth, make time to send notes/emails out to the wonderful GRW (Georgia Romance Writers®) people and new friends I met at the MAGGIES/Moonlight & Magnolias'® conference

It's time to crack my mental whip and get rolling.

BIF, GMC, ABC & 1,2,3

October 30, 2009

My brain is full. For the first time since I forced my butt in a chair to write four and half years ago, I have no idea where to go next with this story.

Last night, for the first time, I told the Physicist I wasn't sure I could pull this story off. Every time I fix X, I find another problem with A, B, C and the list goes on and on. If I change her GMC, I lose his story. If I change his GMC, I lose her story.

It's a nightmare.

My original concept was so fun and light. Now I keep finding great conflicts, but I lose the fun part. I honestly don't see a way out. The Physicist said I needed to look at it abstractly or just write and not worry about it at all. Oddly, I believe the GMC is there. I did like that he had a history where he knew who she was, but she didn't know him at all. Now if I have her know who he is at the beginning, that takes away an element of surprise, too.

It's like knitting with four balls of yarn and hitting a snag, untangling it, and finding a totally different color at the end of the line.

So I sit here, inert. Brain dead. Wondering. Worrying. I'm living in a well of doubt.

Do I scuttle it and lose $50? Write what I originally planned and the heck with the issues facing it? Tweak it and hope for the best in regard to the GH®? Or do I rework it completely and slap the title on the entry even though it no longer suits the story for the GH®? AAAAACCCCKKKKK!!!!!!!!

Yesterday, I read *Break Into Fiction*. The entire thing. Front to back. Great for the next book, and it'll help with this book, but I'm not sure how much I can save. It's like throwing a lifeline to a boat with holes and too many people inside. Someone is going to drown no matter what I do.

I brainstormed. I plotted. I bought sharpie pens. I got poster board. I made gobs of notes.

But now, today, and in this moment? I got nothing. Nada. It's not a writer's block. I can write. I just don't know if what I choose to write will be the right write.

Yesterday, I reread my reasons for writing the story and the original hero/heroine cards I started with and I feel the answer is lurking in them. But where? I have my fishing line out, a hook in the water, and a minnow on the end. But no nibbles are answering my line.

So today. What to do?

I'll play around with it all a bit more. I'll fill out note cards, make my GMC charts, review my brainstorming notes, go through the *Break Into Fiction*© templates a CP sent me, and pray for serious "aha solution moment" to show up between now and Monday.

I'll query another agent with the third MS just to feel some sense of accomplishment.

Resolved to Battle the Demons of Fear & Doubt

January 9, 2012

Usually when I say I will embrace positivity and all things light and wonderful, a serious case of doubt, fear and anxiety follows. Despite knowing that the universe will challenge my resolve, I continue to state my desire to be positive and conquer the beast.

Why? Why do I risk this battle? This battle which will call into question my belief in myself and my drive and my hopes and my dreams?

I wish I had the answer, but I don't. I just know that I do enter into these battles almost as a right of passage. It's as if I must call into question my resolve to succeed in order to prove to myself that I will not let the dark days kill my passion for writing and crafting books.

The Physicist has wisely learned to nod and say nothing when I wage these wars. I will be honest here: I'm not quiet about it. My CPs have learned to let me rant a bit and nod their heads, then say it is the nature of the beast. My beast, my Achilles heel, is my impatience.

I am not patient. I like answers, results, follow through information in a timely manner. That being said, the flip side of this is that I provide all the above in a timely manner. I am fast, efficient, organized, driven, reliable, committed to giving my best. So if you hire me, you'll get a great worker. Or writer (hello? publishing world? can you hear me now?). Give me a deadline and I will meet it barring death or major catastrophe.

Trust me on this. I won't let you down.

But the writing world doesn't operate on Christine Time. It operates on a time wheel, which I have yet to understand. I don't like this time wheel. It's maddening to me. And waiting. Oh, the endless waiting and waiting and waiting drives me insane.

Over the weekend—after embracing positivity—I had a huge meltdown over it. By Sunday I was ready to quit. Yes. Quit. Seven plus years—four of them extremely high paced—of shooting for the stars, the moon, and the sun. Countless dollars spent on conferences, contests, classes, workshops, membership dues, travel, proper clothing, paper, pens, office equipment, gas, hotels, postage. Hours upon hours slaving over stories that might never be read.

It all seemed like a grand waste of my time on Sunday. I ranted about my frustration. My beasts of fear and doubt raged through me and out of me in great bursts. I rebelled. I began shopping on-line. I went to stores and looked at pillows. I did anything BUT the writing.

The Physicist just nodded. He didn't try to fix it (good man that Physicist). The CPs just texted me with little one liners and LOLs and gentle reminders about how I can't control anything but the writing and submitting. And then I came to meet myself in the mirror of all my angst and anger and anxiety.

I said to myself "OK, you've hit the lowest point. Now what? There's nothing else for me folks."

I have to write. I can't not write. I want to win. I will find a new way to achieve my goals while continuing to work on the manuscripts. I will surround myself with positive, loving, understanding people who get me and my dreams. I will not give up despite my weaknesses as a person and a writer.

I do embrace positivity. I also embrace the fact that sometimes I will need more than my own will to get through the dark days. I will need my friends and my support system in place.

Surround yourself with people who support you. Don't just embrace positivity. Embrace people who can be positive for you.

Mental Warfare with Myself: Or How I Beat Myself Back Into the Chair

March 9, 2012

Ah, the inevitable ennui has descended upon me. Part of this is due to travel. Another part is due to worry. The third part is due to a very nicely worded rejection. Not that I'm sad or mad. I like this person. I would like to work with this person. But I have a feeling my voice may not be a match for her. That's okay. Really. Because this is business. There will be someone out there who loves my voice and then the door will open. I will still admire and respect this other person for her honesty.

But the sting still sits under my skin and I am creatively avoiding my revisions. Which isn't good. I'm sort of avoiding them. It seems the closer I get to achieving my dream, the harder it gets to move past the *nos*. I find myself questioning the time and energy I put into this writing deal a lot more.

It's war.

It's me against me.

It's doubt and fear against courage and drive.

So here's how the days start when I am in a mental battle with me. First I lie in bed and I mull over other possible career options that might be easier to accomplish than trying to get published. I've come up with a few:

- Macramé art utilizing spaghetti noodles as the base for the knots.
- Knitting mittens with the leftover spaghetti noodles.
- Stringing pearls onto a necklace that has no knot at the end.
- Capturing mud covered piglets and returning them to their mommas.
- Sewing Tinkerbell's outfits with a small needle and thread.

By the time I get to Tinkerbell, I remember that *All I Need is Faith, Trust, and a little bit of Pixie Dust!*©

As my dear friend and critique partner told me one day after a frenetic round of rejections, if we quit writing we reject ourselves.

So that's it in a nutshell. There are no easy answers. This business is slower than a snake digesting an elephant, and the only thing I have control over is writing and submitting.

Usually by the time I crawl through the mental debris and flack and empty shot shells, I discover a saving grace or a timely note of encouragement or an affirmation that I'm not a total hack.

Bottom line: keep your eye on the prize. One day you will win.

Or die trying.

And that's better than not trying at all.

The Outside World Presses In

April 22, 2013

Writing is a solitary profession. Period. Yes, we can meet with our writing colleagues at meetings and gather at conferences, but for the most part we act alone. No one can write our books for us. No one can revise our first drafts for us. No one can force us to query or submit even when we are filled with doubts about achieving our goals.

Published or unpublished, we all fight demons. For the published authors there are real deadlines. That's great. Puts a fire under one's bottom and presses that author to work.

But me? No one is waiting for me to meet any deadlines right now. So I have to set my own deadlines which, to be honest, have been shifting daily due to outside world pressure and different expectations of myself as a writer.

I'm working hard, but real life has pressed in and I've had to fight for my writing time. Occasionally, I have to surrender to the outside pressure because it's immediate and important and intrinsic to the well-being of my family. Every interruption to my schedule impacts my ability to get back in the chair and diligently pursue a publication career.

Then there are my own demons. Personal ones that every writer, published and unpublished, struggle with all the time. Am I good enough? Have I really got what it takes to write well and write much? Did I say no to an opportunity only to lose the one chance I might have had to be published? Did I start too late? Is the story I'm working on right now good enough? Am I wasting my time? Am I wasting my family's time? Will I ever get paid for sitting here at this computer for hours on end to generate stories and ideas and more?

Do I care about the answers to these questions? Of course I care. However, I live in a delusional, imaginary world so I propose my own answers to these questions all the time. I need to, otherwise I might quit. And if I quit, I reject myself.

Here are my answers: I become a stronger writer every time I sit down to write. I am a self-motivated and self-disciplined person who has the drive to work hard and work smart. There's more than one way to get published and I'm not shy about looking down every avenue. I have a wealth of experience to draw from whenever I sit down to write a story. My current story will become better as I continue to revise it and mold it into shape. If I am happy doing what I am doing, the time I put into it doesn't matter. My family is proud of my endeavors and they support me just as I am proud of their endeavors and support them. I will get paid for generating these stories because I have a plan of action which I am actively pursuing every day.

Inspiration

Remembering Why I Started

November 17, 2008

Today is my dad's birthday. He would have turned eighty-one today had he not passed away six years ago. Losing dad was tough as he was the only parent I had who truly loved me. He influenced me tremendously. From him I developed a love of reading—he was my library connection. When I exhausted all the books at our small town's library, I raided his bookshelves and found The Hobbit (Fourth grade), John Steinbeck and more. From him I learned to be curious and creative and focused on the task at hand.

When I was a child I wanted to be many things: a vet, a movie star (what self respecting girl wouldn't want fame???), and a journalist. I always wrote. Journals, poems, fantasy stories and more. I was fated to write. Yet, as one fellow writer said to me, 'life hijacked me.'

Big time.

I was on my own at sixteen, working as a waitress, and a high school drop out. Writing for a living was not an option, although I never stopped dreaming.

Fast forward to 2002. Married, college educated, a mother, a friend, and still a dreamer. Dad was very ill. The Physicist, my daughter and I traveled to Northern Canada to see him one more time. During that visit, he needed closure. A way to say goodbye and a way to say he was sorry. Part of that regret was due to his failure to protect me from an abusive parent. A parent who didn't want me to succeed, who wanted me to lose my zest for life, who wanted to derail every dream I had as impossible.

I'll never forget when he turned to me with remorse in his timeworn eyes, and said it was *too late for me to be a writer*. At the time, I believed him. I had laid my dream to rest and was pursuing the idea of becoming a personal life coach. Heck, I am an enthusiastic person, and I've encouraged so many people in achieving their dreams, I figured why not get paid for it? I absolved him of his own guilt and said it was okay. I was okay. I really was doing great.

But the dream that had lain dormant resurrected on that day. And a few months later, I trotted out an old half started manuscript, and I finished it! I sent it off in a query and, fantastically, got a request. No. The story doesn't end with a published novel. No. The first book I wrote is not that great and will never be published. However, it will never be forgotten. It is the first book I wrote. I proved to myself it was not too late for me to write. Since that first book churned out of me, I have written two other books.

On Dad's birthday, I wish I could say to him that it's not too late. That I am a writer. I will, with a lot of luck and hard work, be published one day.

Catching Waves

October 8, 2009

We're at the beach. My family and I are on a huge, well-deserved break. But as I was watching the waves, going into the water and catching the waves, a recent keynote address by the famous Sherrilyn Kenyon washed through my mind.

In this keynote address, poignant and oh, so very real, she said she stopped chasing trends. She wanted to be published so very badly. Heck, she'd been published. Six books! But now she was chasing dreams, living a life she wishes on no one, and desperate. She wrote book after book, chasing trends in the writing industry. Nothing stuck. Then she wrote a Regency novel with the help of her critique partners, and sent it off.

It was rejected. It was a horrible rejection.

But it managed to accomplish one thing. It put Ms. Kenyon back on the right road. She stopped chasing trends, and she started writing the books in her heart. Those are the NYT (New York Times) best sellers we see on the shelves today. She followed her heart, she wrote the books in her heart, and she sold the books. She told each and every one of us at the Moonlight and Magnolias Conference, to stop chasing trends, never quit, and keep writing. Write the books in our hearts.

Today I thought about that as I waited on the sandbar for waves with my daughter. It was so tempting to chase the waves cresting just to the left or the right. But I remembered, don't chase trends. I translated that to *don't chase the waves*. We're in the water, we're waiting, and we're doing all the right things, a wave will come and we will catch it.

That is what writing and pursuing publishing is for me. I am in the writing water. I am waiting, and I am doing all the right things. I want to chase that elusive dream, follow that trend... I think it's urban fantasy... but that's not my story to tell. I have to hold back. I have to wait. I have to wait for the right wave to catch and surf into the beach.

It's hard to wait. But I am in the water, I am doing all the right things, and I will catch the right wave.

Be true to your muse. You're in the writing water. You might not know it, but your wave might be right around the corner.

Are you ready?

Will you catch it?

Will you ride it home?

I plan to be writing, submitting, waiting, writing, entering contests, and waiting. I plan to be in my water. I plan to write my stories.

I will catch my wave. I don't know when it will arrive. But I plan to be ready!

Reading: A Lost Art of the Writer

December 5, 2009

Today I worked on my MS. I fiddled with a scene, printed out the rest of the WIP, internalized some ideas (not all great—worry abounds), and then I allowed myself reading time. No, not reading contest entries. Not reading blogs (though I love them). Not reading forums and loops to stay in the know. Not reading craft books (though that's on my to-do list). Nope. I attempted reading for pleasure.

Remember that concept, my writing friends? Reading for pleasure. Reading for the sheer joy of being immersed in a book and loving the characters and just flipping the pages until you reached 'the end?' Ah, that's why I became a writer. I love to read.

I used to be a proverbial book slut. There's no other way of putting it. I read any and all genres, non-fiction and fiction. I read classics by Wilkie

Collins and Willa Cather and Bronte. I read pulp fiction. I read Fantasy. I read Romances. I read self-help books. I read Inspirational books. I read Westerns (yes I did). I read children's books. I read Young Adult books. I read cheap thrillers. I read Mysteries.

I read a lot.

Now I write. There's barely time to read a published book unless it's a new author I want to support or a book about writing. I do read at night with my reading glasses perched on my face and my brain weary. I fall asleep with the glasses on my nose and the book on the floor (will a KINDLE survive my abuse? Doubtful). *(May 2105 Note: I own a Kindle, a Nook, and an iPad. They are my first sources for reading. They've survived being read by me.)*

I read books in my genre and pick them apart. When did she hook me? Or how did he make me turn the pages? How long are the scenes? Where are the PPPs? And on and on.But today I tried to 'read for pleasure.' It was hard at first. Really hard. I kept counting pages and scene lengths (uh, I am thinking of going to Single Title length and this book's a ST, RS). I kept looking and marveling at how the authors had spun the tale so beautifully (and comparing it to my own crap writing—still having a bit of a PPP here). I had the most difficult time just getting into the story.

But it happened. Slowly. I did just start flipping the pages and enjoying the sheer joy of being transported into another world and not worrying about the technique and the pacing and the plot. I just read.

Fictional People

January 10, 2010

Developing people who pop off the pages and live in a reader's mind isn't an easy task. There are dozens of ways to build characters and give them depth. I've employed many methods, but I am by no means an expert. If I were, maybe I'd already be published.

But I am learning and growing as a writer and this is becoming easier with each new book I write. Hmmm, maybe not 'easier,' but I'm recognizing my mistakes more quickly and rectifying them either as I write my current WIP, or as I plan for the next MS.

My Character Illumination from Donald Maass's book *Writing the Breakout Novel*:

Developing fictional people is mainly a matter of opening oneself to real people, mostly ourselves.

Writers are often portrayed as reclusive personalities. In years past, the writer was also portrayed as cynical, bitter and anti-social.

Do I fit the mold? Nope. I think most of the writers I know aren't anti-social and reclusive. Oh, we have to work many solitary hours and God forbid anyone bang on my office door when I am in the middle of hammering out a solution to a difficult scene, but most of us enjoy our peeps in the real world, too.

We're certainly not all quiet and shy beings, either. I am a talker, social and flitting around the social scene. I do thrive on people and interactions with them. I chat a lot, but I also ask questions. I listen. I hear the nuances. I bet most writers do listen. Where else do we get 'voice?'

For instance, I spent a good deal of time chatting with the Physicist's Aunt B when we went to Texas to see his father. Aunt B was a true character. Funny, opinionated, loving, caring and addicted to QVC. She heralded me with her stories about her shopping online for her Christmas gifts. About how she explained them to her husband. She showed me all her jewelry acquired through her shopping efforts.

But underlying her cute stories was a deeper story. One of loss. First, her grown son to cancer, suddenly and inexplicably. Then her other son's escapades with marriage. And her husband's sudden battle with cancer (hey, that's when the QVC shopping began). Now her brothers, the Physicist's dad and uncle, are ill and they are dying. And she is eager for connection with us, with anyone.

That's the depth. Her humor, her character and her love all shine.

If I only talked, never listened, I'd not know the depth of her stories.

That's what being in the real world is for me. It's filled with real people, their voices, their stories, their hurts, their outrages, their pain, their betrayals, their judgments and their histories. I listen. I bring to the table of my writing my own set of pain and betrayal and joy and history.

During the 2009 RWA® National Conference®, keynote speaker Eloisa James said, "Mine yourself, mine your emotions. Pour yourself into the characters you are creating. They are born of you." (Paraphrased)

Learn writing craft, practice writing everyday, but most of all be in the world. Pour yourself into people, learn their worlds and share of yourself. Be real in the world and your people will be real in your fictional world.

Perseverance, or an Obsessive Stubborn Refusal to Give Up?

June 1, 2010

I've been reading a lot of blogs about the writer's life. How do we sit in the chair, often without pay, to write these stories? Why do we sit in the chair at all? How does one know if a writer, new and unpublished, will become successful?

Is it perseverance or an obsessive stubborn refusal to give up on one's dream? Or is it a combination of both qualities along with a measure of self-delusion about the difficulty in achieving the ultimate dream of publication?

Perseverance defined:

Noun: steadfastness in doing something despite difficulty or delay in achieving success: her perseverance with the technique illustrates her single mind.

Perseverance with the technique stands out for me.

Read it again. It says, *try try try* again but with the technique.

If we sit in a chair and write every day, meeting our word count goals and more, then yes, we're persevering. We often do it without affirmation or pay. It's even harder to persevere if we don't have a paycheck or an editor breathing down our necks for our works.

I believe writing and making writing goals is not enough. I believe that we need to learn, and that we need to persevere with our technique. We are never finished with the process of learning, regardless of where we are on our writing journey.

Persevere with your technique. Accept constructive feedback, take courses about writing, ask for help, read books in your genre, attend workshops, enter contests, find a critique partner you trust (I've been super lucky in that regard), and when you say, "Never Give Up, Never Surrender," you're saying it as you steadfastly work toward refining your technique.

What are you doing to achieve your goal? How are you accepting the changes you need to make as a writer so you can step inside the hallowed halls of publication? Don't just write. Write with purpose, with a willingness to grow and change. As you struggle with the difficult tasks you face as a writer, try to remember why you embarked on this journey.

Rediscover daily the joy you have as a writer. The sheer amazing wonderful way your heart sings when you put words onto paper. Then become a master, an empress, of your joy and harness it with knowledge and technique.

Driving Lessons

June 4, 2010

My daughter is learning to drive. I've been her primary teacher for a few months. I remember the first time I took her out. There are claw marks on the door handle! But with each trip out, she's gotten better and more confident. I believe I've managed to get through the experience without getting too many gray hairs. My door handle is starting to return to its original shape as I become more relaxed with her sitting behind the wheel. In addition to my personal lessons, we've paid for her summer school driving lessons. Today she gets behind the wheel of a huge Ford Expedition.

Fortunately for the people at large, she is not leaving the parking lot until Monday.

She's nervous about driving a different car. I don't blame her. Driving is a scary deal until you master it. Even then, despite many years of experience, driving is potentially dangerous, even deadly. The most experienced driver is no match for the inexperienced or incapacitated driver.

It occurred to me that learning to drive is much like mastering the writing craft. How?

- You can't go anywhere until you switch on the ignition and turn on the car. You can't become a writer until you stop talking about doing it and you start actually putting words on paper. How many people have you met who 'are going to write a book?' How many of those people have written a book? Talk is cheap, switch on your writing ignition and get started.

- You can't go anywhere until you put the car into DRIVE and move forward. If you are writing and you're not submitting your work, you aren't going to get anywhere. You'll be stuck in your writing driveway with a manuscript. You have got to get your work out of the garage and send it somewhere. You have got to risk rejection just as a driver has to risk the road if you wish to reach your destination.

- Driving is a skill you must master one step at a time. You can't become the next NYT best seller until you hone you craft and build your skills. I am not the writer I was four and a half years ago when I wrote my first manuscript. I hope to be a much better writer than I am in five years. How? Practice! Practice writing every day and you will become a better writer.

- People drive at different speeds. Some people hit the accelerator and reach their destinations fast. Other people go too fast and they crash and burnout. Some people go very slow and watch other cars go around them, but eventually they might get there. Other people follow the speed limit. They are less likely to crash and most likely to reach their destination at the right time. My dad used to say, "Better late, than never." I agree. Find your comfortable writing pace. Go at your speed limit. You will get there.
- No matter how skilled, drivers are not guaranteed a safe ride. There is always danger and problems you will encounter along the way. Potholes, road rage, poor road management, other accidents along the way, flat tires, no gas stations to refuel—they are all out there. Be aware of the dangers and pitfalls when you get behind the wheel and prepare for them mentally. Writers must refuel, dodge negativity, fill their minds with positive thoughts, avoid creating negativity and prepare for all possibilities.
- There are always detours when you're driving. The same can be said about writing. Life happens. Sometimes the detours offer a better, different way to reach your destination. Be willing to adjust your driving and writing goals. Be willing to adjust the way you believe you will get to your destination. Everybody has a different,

unique way of reaching their goals and destinations. Be flexible about how you will reach your destination.

Today my daughter is getting into a Ford Expedition and learning how to park, perform turns and more. Next week she will be out on the road with five other teenagers (God bless the coaches who are teaching them!). In a year she'll be driving her own vehicle to school. If I hadn't sat in the car with her for that first lesson, in the church parking lot, with my hand gripping the door and my heart lodged in my throat, she would not have the confidence or skills to drive.

Don't be afraid to take chances on yourself. Write your stories, send them out into the world, keep learning how to write and improve your craft. Develop your skills and confidence will naturally grow out of that development. Don't forget to enjoy the scenery along the way as you drive toward achieving your dream.

Busy-ness Can Lead to Dizzy-ness

June 9, 2010

People's lives are busy. Some people actually define their lives by saying, "I'm so busy, or too busy or these are busy days." They revel in the busy-ness of their lives. They revel in the going out and about to do a zillion errands, or projects, or luncheons. They revel in being seen as 'busy.' Busy-ness defines their lives.

But sometimes I wonder if these people who are so *busy* are actually just avoiding themselves. Avoiding personal introspection. Avoiding examining who they are or where they need to go. Other times I wonder if these busy people are busy because it makes them feel important. The busy-ness defines them.

Ever met somebody like that? I've met a few. I may have actually been guilty of committing the act of *busy-ness* myself. Heck, I was young once. I did my fair share and plus of extra work when I was employed outside the home and afterward. I remember an incredibly intense time after I became a mom where I spent about six or seven years volunteering in the school, the church, the neighborhood—basically did it all. For free. But then I think part of my motivation was the free babysitting *grin*.

I was a *busy* person. And I knew a lot of *busy people*. It wasn't until I was forced to sit down and take stock that I truly began my inner journey. I admit that I was a self-help book addict for years. Heck, with the crazy dysfunctional background I came from, who wouldn't be? But I never really examined who I wanted to be until I couldn't be out in the world being, well, you know, 'busy.'

Yup. I couldn't be busy cause I got this weirdo bug in my ear that made me dizzy. Beyond dizzy. I had a serious case of perpetual vertigo. It was the kind of vertigo that made me sick, blackout, with tremendous heat and frightening moments of disorientation. The only way to beat it back was to stop being so busy.

I was brought down by a tiny bug, which had lodged in my inner ear for six months.

At first I was so sick, and I didn't have much energy. I napped. Me taking a nap was unheard of in my house. I am a *get up and go* kinda girl. Naturally, after I had a few months of serious downtime, I got bored. You know boredom is actually not a bad thing. Boredom means you're healing. Boredom means your mind is getting ready for the next creative adventure.

Now if a *get up and go* girl can't really, uh, go anywhere in the real world, what is she going to do? Oh, hmmm, any good guesses out there? Oh, yeah. Write. That's how I rediscovered what I know I was always meant to do. I began writing my first novel. It was an escape, a joyful experience, and I fell in love with my childhood dreams again.

That was a wonderful year. The said book was finished, queried and requested by a major romance publishing house's line before I even knew about Romance Writers of America®, Craft, and more.

Fast forward almost five years. I'm still focused on the writing. I love it. I have four books under my belt (though I call them 8 given all the recent plot revisions) and I am submitting, being requested, and happily involved in all my RWA®/PRO/Chapter organizations. I am also blogging, Facebook connecting (imagine if they'd had Facebook back when I first got dizzy? I might not be writing cause I'd be *busy* connecting with my social network), Tweeting, helping with an online workshop, volunteering to help with the PRO Retreat, judging contests, entering contests.... YIKES! I am afraid I might get dizzy again.

Yes, before you ask, I am blonde. Let the jokes begin and end now.

But I won't get dizzy. You know why I believe in my heart I won't get dizzy? All my *busy* stuff is what I want to do for my career (and my family—which comes first). I have learned the fine art of saying *no*. Or, better, *let me get back to you about that request after I think about it.* Or better yet, *I would like some help with this please.*

Most of all, I've given myself permission to walk away from my commitments and take a breath. When dinner starts, if the phone rings, I don't answer it. Period. I keep my commitments to a set amount and I don't feel obligated to be perfect (losing perfectionism is a great way to give up the *busy* life). I don't say *yes* to make someone think better of me. I don't say *yes* to gain approval or puff up my ego. Frankly, I don't consider saying *yes* to anything that does not reflect my Top 5 Priority List.

Ah, the Top 5 Priority List. I learned about this method of establishing boundaries from a book called <u>*Life Makeover*</u> by Cheryl Richardson that I read when I was dizzy. I reevaluate it every quarter. Usually it stays the same, or at least the top two items stay the same. The bottom three items vary depending on season, where I am in my life, and how the rest of the family is faring.

But what is a priority? What does this word mean to you? Here is a brief dictionary explanation:

Priority Defined:

Noun:

- A thing that is regarded as more important than another.

  The housework didn't figure high on her list of priorities.

  Seriously? It never does figure high on my list of priorities. Sure I want to prevent my toilets from being deemed toxic and hazardous, but if my house is dirty and you want to come over cause you're down or need a friendly face, I'm your girl!

- The fact or condition of being regarded or treated as important.
  The safety of the country takes priority over every other matter.

  Or, the health and welfare of my family, and myself, is regarded or treated as important. If I am trying to do too much, everyone suffers, including me.

- The right to take precedence or proceed before others.
  Priority is given to those with press passes.

  Now I love this. The items/things/people who take precedence or proceed before others in my life are my family first, my writing (actual writing, not blogging or stuff of that nature), my health, my dearest friends, my spirit and my soul. Everybody and everything else must wait in line. Period.

This getting your priorities straight isn't a perfect process. Sometimes I revert and nibble a bit more off than I can chew. Usually the first thing that suffers is my health. So I get a pretty quick reminder to get my priorities sorted.

Ironically, my weirdest time to keep my priorities straight is through the summer months. I've got these writing goals, but I scale them back a bit, or make room for flexible writing time, during this time of year. My daughter is underfoot, we've got summer travel plans, and I want to enjoy my family during these lazy days. I don't stop writing, but I do break it up differently. My priority is to work on my MS or WIP in Revision. If I'm not on

Facebook or other social media that means I'm focusing on my first priority: health and happiness of my family. We're probably at the pool, or shopping, or visiting some museum. That's okay.

That's the key to maintaining your priorities and boundaries: telling yourself it's okay to let something slide or go slack every once in a while. Really!

Dear Books I've Written—I Owe You A New Look

June 11, 2010

Dear Christine's Books,

I have been busy revising my fourth book (you know who you are and we'll talk later), and I've been making my plans for my next two Contemporary Romances tickling the idea center of my brain. But I've been rude and I have forgotten to remember you, my first three books, in all my pushing forward and planning for my future.

First of all, you might want to know that it was one of our CPs who reminded me about you. She suggested that I go back and take a look at all of you again and transform you into contenders in the writing world. What? I thought about it. Why would I want to face you all again? I was 'just learning.' I didn't even revise number one or number two (once I believed copy editing was revising—laugh now). But she suggested I review you all again, think about entering you into contests after I tweak you into shape based on all I have learned.

Interesting idea. You know what? I agree.

Number three? You've been resurrected already. I had all but buried you when the same CP said, "rename your book and enter it into the MAGGIE® again." Now you're on your way to two other contests and I've submitted you to a publishing house. Woohoo. Where will those submissions lead? Who knows? But I am glad we're working together again.

Number two? Oh, I was so proud of you when I finished you. I had a structured plot, a virgin (haha), a big story and I set it in Canada. According to a writer I met from Canada at last year's RWA® National Conference, Canadian settings don't sell. What the heck, eh? That might be true, but I have news for you. You're going back out there. I'll change the setting to reflect this interesting tidbit of information and send you back into the gauntlet. We can do this. Really. We can. You deserve a chance.

And now my Number one manuscript you are the first book of my heart. The one I wrote with joy, freedom and an absolute lack of understanding about POV (Point of View) changes within a scene being verboten. Well darling, I am going to give you another chance. You deserve it. You taught me that I had the power within me to make my dream come alive. You made me a writer. Thank you for that gift. I want to give you another chance.

You see, my darling books, I have a tendency to cut my losses and move forward rather quickly. If at first I don't succeed, I try again with another book. Oh, I know all about revision now (thank you book number three and number four for that lovely lesson). I know I have to keep producing new material, but I had moved forward believing the old was useless. For that thought, I owe you an apology.

You are not useless. You are my first books. You have potential. I have grown as a writer with each and every one of you. Book One? You restored my childhood dreams. Book Two? You enriched my understanding about the craft of writing. Book Three? You validated my writing when you finaled in the 2009 MAGGIE®, and when you were requested many times. Wow. Proud moments. Happy moments.

Book Four? You continue to make me stretch out of my comfort zone and you've taught me to understand how to approach my next book. Thank you for making me face the one person in my life I never addressed emotionally in my prior books. I love you for that gift.

So my darling books, we are going to head into the next months of writing with a renewed commitment. I'm redressing you in finer clothes and sending you back out into the world. You're going to travel again to contests and publishers and agents. It's time to up the ante and challenge myself to pursue my dreams in a new way.

Now a brief note to my as yet unwritten books. You know who you are. I will write you. I will begin plotting book five after RWA® Nationals. I'll write the first draft before October rolls around (thank God I am a fast first draft writer). We'll journey forward. You'll be a part of my collection of arrows. Arrows I am sending out into the world every chance I get.

Thank you my books. Thank you from the bottom of my heart for your creative and intellectual gifts to me.

Love,
Christine

Good Intentions Are Paving Stones

June 21, 2010

Good intentions. Everyone's got them. What do we do with them? My father used to say, "the road to hell is paved with good intentions." He probably heard or read that statement from somewhere/some famous person, but I always attribute the phrase to my dad. I heard him say it a lot (usually after I had failed to clean my room, wash the dishes, sweep the floor, etc.—what can I say? I am a sloth).

Let me tell you, being grounded for intending to do something and then not accomplishing it is a little like being in the pits of hell.

But being a kid who fails to follow through on a promised chore who is grounded is not the same as being an adult who intends to become, to do, to be anything and then the adult fails to follow through on her intent. The resulting hell is not filled with brimstone and fire and a man wearing a bizarre red cape who pokes you with a pitchfork.

The hell is one's own sense of worth going down the toilet. Flushed. Gone. The man with the pitchfork is really one's conscious saying, "you're a failure and a loser." Ouch. That's a pretty big poke in the head, right?

Here's what else that dude in the cape who lives in your head says (I don't care what religion, or not, a person is—we all have egos and a conscious capable of creating this negativity), "You may as well not bother to intend to do anything again cause you will not succeed. Just quit before you start." Bigger blow to the psyche, right?

What is the solution? Do not intend to do anything unless you plan to carry through on your intention. You're writing a book? You want to write a book? You intend to write a book? Then write the darned book. Don't tell yourself you'll fail before you start writing or while you're writing. Regardless of your religion or lack of one, I think that's the dang man with the pitch fork talking. Really. It is. If you fail to become who you were intended to be, then that dude in the cape wins.

Now in this case, I use writing the darned book because that's what I'm geared up to do. That's my desire and my intent. I am fulfilled by the action of carrying through on my intention. The end result is a happy and satisfied me. The rest is gravy, icing, cherries, you name it. But I have the substance. I have the full satisfaction one feels after eating a super wonderful meal that's been plated up for me to enjoy.

As long as I live the life intended for me, carry through on using my gifts and talents to the best of my ability then I am in a place called heaven. Finding heaven on earth is a great discovery.

You Don't Know What You Don't Know

June 27, 2010

I'm on vacation and part of the time I'm away I'm staying with my dear friend in Oakton, VA. Her mother is a super person and has come along to the pool with us (along with dear friend's daughters aged four and six) as we hang out. It's been fun not having a regular schedule, floating through the lazy days of summer vacation with young children, smelling the scent of chlorine and sun block lotion. Playing games, coloring and reading stories is always a fun treat for this mom of a teen. The hosts are beyond generous and super people.

As the lazy days progress, I have managed to write a little here and there, but I've been taking in life at a gentler pace, too. That means getting into interesting conversations with interesting people like my dear friend and her parents. Her mother brought up a New York Times series that dear friend's sister had forwarded to her: a series about the concept *You don't know what you don't know*. We've had a lot of fun with the play on words, but based on our conversations, it's really about the human ability to deny the existence of a problem before they undertake something or to not know what problems lie ahead of their efforts to perform some task.

Okay, she used a bank robber who believed if he rubbed lemon juice on his face, no one would see his face in a photograph. He didn't know what he didn't know. Obviously or he wouldn't have attempted his bone headed attempt to rob a bank with lemon juice on his face. I know that lemon juice doesn't prevent my face from being recognized. I know what I know. But had I known five years ago what I know now, would I have begun writing?

I didn't know what I didn't know. I didn't know how hard it was to get published. I didn't know how painful it was to revise. I didn't know how frustrating the task of unthreading a story multiple times and sewing it back together again would be to perform. I didn't know how much I had to know about plot, craft, POV. I didn't know about RWA®, writing chapters, and online writing classes. I didn't know that I would stop doing everything I was into doing to give my heart to writing.

I didn't know what I didn't know. I didn't know I'd meet amazing people who didn't know what they didn't know. I didn't know that I'd grow tough skin and learn to deal with rejections. I didn't know that I had more than one story in me. I didn't know that I had something to offer other writers as a reader, a judge, a friend, and a motivator. I didn't know what I didn't know.

I'm glad I didn't know what I didn't know. If I had known about the hard stuff, I might not have started writing. Then I wouldn't have learned about all the wonderful, good stuff about writing.

I'm sure I don't know what I don't know about many more things. I'll leave the gathering of the knowledge to time, experience and the pursuit of knowledge.

Mission Confirmed: Write My Own Story My Way

October 4, 2010

This weekend I attended the Moonlight and Magnolias Conference® hosted by the Georgia Romance Writers®. My writing friend and I managed to survive our trip of four plus hours with little incident (uh, there was that weird pick up line by an unwashed person in McDonalds and a strange toothless person who quite liked my buddy and a wild animal chaser running across the freeway, but I am happy to report no lives were lost during the incident.... but I digress—come on a road trip with us one day and have fun).

But here's the deal: all these adventures are worth the end result for me. First, I bond with a fabulous writing friend as we discuss our writing, life, and the universe. Then I get to hang out with amazing authors, writers and workshop leaders. I get to celebrate the MAGGIES®.

So first up, I attended the workshops. Allison Brennan doesn't plot and I LOVE her for that!! But what I really love is this wisdom: write YOUR story YOUR WAY. Michael Hauge's workshop was about plot and structure and the hero's journey and I learned so much my head ached by the end of the day. But here's what I really learned beyond my ah ha moment about the yin and yang of the conflict of false ego running from true essence as revealed by relationship with another who sees one for who she/he is inside: I learned to believe that I deserve to win.

My epiphany. My story. My end result. Someone else might have another one. But this was mine. I own it.

Finally, I took a workshop about goal setting given by Kelly Stone. Hmmm. I always set goals, so what could I learn? But I learned I had limited my goal setting. I set them by the year and break them down. Now? Oh, wow. I set them by 20 years, by 10 years, by 5 years. I want to see what it will taste like. It will be good. It will change. It will be fluid. But it will be good. Why? It is my story told my way in my time and I am stoked.

Okay, so I am on a conference high. On a little *ah, I got a first place in the Emerald City Opener Contest® and a second place in the same contest* high. Yeah, and I might have had a bit of chocolate. Oh, some champagne. Oh. Yeah. Some dancing occurred, too. All good.

But at the end of the day, here is what is really wonderful. I have a fortune cookie fortune in my jewelry box that I have kept for quite a while. It says: *Your ability to find the silly in the serious will take you far.*

This is my voice! Seriously. I mean it. A cookie fortune has pegged my voice in a nutshell. Or perhaps in a cookie shell? Whatever. This is me. This is my voice. This is my story. I have the ability to find the silly in the serious, and it will take me far.

Blogger Oz

October 11, 2010

I've just finished taking an amazing social media class with Kristen Lamb. I've learned a thing or two about branding myself (ouch, that could hurt), and social networking because of this class. Ouch again, I have decided to retool my blog space to reflect the lessons.

Super ouch again because I am also going to *gulp* learn more about social media and branding myself via a book I ordered. Kristen Lamb's book, *We Are Not Alone*: *The Writer's Guide to Social Media* is recommended by editors and agents to newly contracted authors. *(May 2015 Note: The blog and book are no longer available via the links I used to have which is unfortunate. Google Kristen Lamb and see if you can find this very informative woman online.)*

I'm not contracted yet. But I had better learn how to use social media to sell my books and my name if I want to make it in this business. The writing world is huge, the business is changing every day, and I need to get savvy about utilizing this free network.

I have dabbled in it before, but never pushed too hard because social media can suck up a lot of time. Facebook is not for playing farmer games or finding treasure. Well, in a way it is. I'm farming for future readers and digging for future treasure in sales the day my book hits shelves finally arrives.

Yes, dear readers, the contest definitely brought the concept of self-promotion home to me. If I want to sell books, sell novels, and sell my stories I have to be bold, fearless and courageous about marketing.

I'm not in Kansas anymore. Oz is a bit frightening. There are a lot of wild characters and new lands to explore. There are wild colors, terms I don't understand, witches and wizards of writing promotion to conquer. Oh, I am nervous. But I am not going to crawl back into the back corner of the house I just flew in to get here and hide from the experience. I'm going to embrace it.

During his workshop at the Georgia Romance Writers'® Moonlight and Magnolias Conference® Conference, Michael Hauge asked each writer to examine her/himself in terms of this question: I'll do anything to be a published writer except (fill in the blank) because THAT'S NOT ME.

I can fill in that blank. Before that workshop, I could say, *I'll do anything to be a published author except self promote because that's not me.* It's not. Not totally. After all, that's called 'drawing attention to oneself' and I have my own reasons for not wanting to do that. Sure, those who know me will say I am outgoing and gregarious. But if you really spend time with me, you'll notice that what I am actually doing is getting people to talk about themselves. I'm promoting other people to draw attention away from myself.

Good self-preservation trick, eh?

Now all this eye-opening self-awareness at a deeper level than I had ever examined of myself before isn't going to stop me from continuing to motivate and encourage the people I love and admire to achieve their goals as writers, mothers, sisters, brothers, fathers, husbands, students.... ah the list goes on. It's an amazing feeling to see the people around me grow and become who they have the potential to be in this great glorious life. I'm just adding one more person to the list. Me.

Get Your Groove On-
Motivation Comes from Within

October 15, 2010

I'm an unpublished writer. There's no pay, no glory other than the occasional contest final or win, and there's no one beating down the door to read my novels (except for my critique partners). But I write. I sit down in front of a computer screen and type away for hours with no end in sight. I write my stories, submit them to contests, query them to agents and editors, win or lose contests, get rejected. But I persist. I persist despite life happening all around me. I know other writers who persist despite the odds.

We are an exceptional breed.

Kelly Stone said that there are research studies performed on writers: we're motivated high achievers according to the researchers. I say we're delusional, masochistic, optimistic dreamers. I believe we're not the only subset of people, the ones who write and finish books, who persist despite the odds.

This idea isn't just for writers. It is for anyone who wants to accomplish something and has to do so in a vacuum. Or a mini vacuum. You can be a student, an artist, a decorator, a mother (last of the unsung heroes in my opinion), a cancer patient fighting to live and go on—the list goes on.

I have learned to motivate myself. Why? I grew up in a household where I wasn't encouraged to succeed. If anything, I was encouraged to fail (but that's a women's fiction story that I really think would bore most readers—who hasn't got some dysfunction in their lives, right?). But I managed to put myself through modeling school, get my GED/High school equivalency certificate, study for the SATs on my own and score over 1100 back in the day, go to college and graduate with a 4.0 and at the top of the Dean's List.

No one did this for me. No one cheered for me. Years later a mom of a friend said to me, "You really did accomplish a lot and you should be very proud." I appreciate her words so much. Up until then I had really just had the attitude that the job had to be done so I did it.

Apparently, I am an exception to the rule.

I want to make you an exception to the rule.

If you're a writer, a painter, a mother, a student, a (fill in the blank), then it's time to embrace your dream and go for it.

Make time to perform your duty/seek out your Golden Grail.

In other words, don't just talk about doing this wonderful thing you are about to do. I can't tell you how many people I have met who say to me they are also 'going to write a book' when they learn I am an unpublished writer. I can't tell you how many of them want me to write their love story of pain and loss and victory or just loss. But they're just talking. They're not doing.

You can't do what you want to do if you are only talking about doing it.

You must sit down and do it.

How? You say you don't have huge chunks of time to do this thing you want to do? I strike down this opposition. You have a half an hour? You have time.

You'd be amazed how much you can accomplish in just half an hour.

Try it. Schedule half an hour a day at least five days a week to perform your thing that you want to do. Or to prepare to do that thing that you want to do. Half an hour. That's thirty minutes away from Facebook, surfing the Internet, or emailing videos to friends.

You want to go to medical school but haven't applied? Apply!! You want to paint a picture, but don't know how? Call a craft store and find out if they have classes. You want to learn to cook like the amazing Julia Child? Take a class, buy the book, start cooking. You want to write (I know you are out there reading this), close down the web server and turn on your word processor. Don't have a story? An idea? Start writing. You'd be amazed at how quickly the universe opens up for you and sends you a story.

There are no excuses allowed in my world. If I can write through a father-in-law dying of cancer, the Physicist having hip replacement surgery, health problems and more, then you can do what it is you have to do. When the Physicist had his hip replacement, I didn't even force myself to write a half an hour. I told myself to write every day. Yes, there were days that I only wrote a sentence or a paragraph, but there were also days where I wrote pages and pages.

I wrote. I finished the book.

What do you want to do? Do you have half an hour to do it? Do you have more than half an hour? Go for it. What is the worst thing that can happen? You fail? You flop? Your writing never gets published? So what? At least you can say you gave it an effort. You're success is truly in the effort given to the project. All the rest of it? The As, the certificates, the money, the fame (yeah, let's dream about it), the careers—they're byproducts of our efforts.

My daughter's middle school principal told her eighth grade graduating class that their group was the first group he'd seen come through his doors in over seven years that had so much potential. They did. He wasn't just saying these words year after year. All the teachers, the counselors and the parents knew this group was special. Something was in the water that year. This group was by far one of the most empathetic, giving and supportive wave of students they had walking through the doors. I have my theories about why. They were in the 2nd grade during 9/11 in the DC area. They were in the 3rd grade during the sniper attacks and had to rely on adults to protect them. They had no recess for 6 weeks, and they had to practice shelter in place in case of biological warfare attacks. They had to trust their teachers and each other and other parents. They developed a level of empathy in young people I have yet to witness again. They are a unique group. I know I will see many of them become stellar adults in this crazy world we live in today.

But here is what else this principal said. "Potential without perseverance and persistence is pointless." Now is the time when you must ask yourself what you are willing to do to get the job done. Develop your potential. Grow. Learn. Apply. Do. You cannot just be a lump of clay. You must become the vessel that holds the water that nourishes the thirsty.

Work for It. Develop Your Talents. Strive to Win.

October 29, 2010

You've embarked on a journey toward a goal. One you believe in and want to achieve. You tell someone about your dream. That person laughs, asks if you are crazy, rains on your parade and tells you it is unattainable.

Now, if you are a seventy year old and you've just told your wife you're thinking about becoming a circus high wire act despite the fact that you have no coordination then you might deserve the above scenario.

Yes, dreams should be realistically attainable.

If your dream is realistically attainable, and someone in your life says you shouldn't try to attain this dream, then you need to reevaluate your relationship with that person.

Tip for the Day: Surround yourself with positive, supportive people as you pursue your dream.

I wrote about my own journey from solitary writer to writer with a wealth of support. I've heard the negative comments. One close relative said, "You'll never get published" when I told her I was writing a book. Do I share my dreams with her now? No way because I believe I will get that call. But it's more than my own faith in my dream. I want the people in my life to be excited for me because I'm doing something I love. It feeds my soul in ways that I never expected. The end result? Publication? That's just part of the dream. I am living my dream. I am a writer. I write. I am happy because I am writing.

Here's the thing: people who are negative about your dreams and your goals aren't happy so they don't want you to be happy either.

Trust me. I've learned this lesson and it has served me well. I repeat: when someone is mean or nasty to you and rains on your parade that person doesn't want you to be happy and fulfilled.

I am writing because it brings me joy. Sure there are days that I want to drop kick my laptop to the ends of the earth. I get frustrated. I feel the sting of rejection and throw personal pity parties (for a finite amount of time), but I keep on writing because that is when my positive community of support comes into play. These are the people who remind me about how much fun it is to do what I do. They encourage me. They lift my spirits. They make me laugh. They drink wine and eat dark chocolate with me while they tell me you will succeed.

Surround yourself with positive peers who celebrate your dream and encourage you to keep working hard to attain the prize you seek. These are the people who must be in your world as you pursue your dreams. They are the people who want you to be happy and fulfilled. They are the people who want you to have joy in your life.

When you reach your dream? They will be first in line to celebrate your victory!

Dive In and Start Swimming

November 5, 2010

I once had the privilege of hearing Nora Roberts speak at the Romance Writers of America® National Conference. She was the keynote luncheon speaker, and she gave an Author Chat later that day, too. Her books are too many to count and she is very dedicated to her career.

What's her secret? Just write.

What's her message to people who give excuses and stay on the sidelines? Get in the pool and start swimming.

This message is true for anyone pursuing any activity or goal. If you want to do something and achieve something, please don't make excuses for not doing it. This is just another way of avoiding the possibility of failure. We've all been there. We've all failed. The trick is to move beyond the failure and keep on trying.

Here's my tip for the week: Whenever you hear yourself saying, "I'd like to do this but...." turn around the phrase and say, "Even though this situation exists, I am going to push myself to work toward my goal anyway."

Here's some wonderful excuses I've heard whenever I hear people say they'd like to write a book, or they could write a book, or how easy it is to write a book if only....

They'd do what I've done if only they had enough time. They'd do what I've done if only they didn't have a day job. I've got friends who work full time and write and raise families. Somehow they manage to make the time. They'd do what I've done if only they had no health problems, no people tugging for their attention, no family members sick, no... no... no...

Hmmmm. I see a pattern here. A pattern punctuated by one word. The word *no* is ringing in my ears. If only? *If only* is another way of saying *no*. *But* is another way of saying *no*.

Turn this around. Tell yourself *yes*. Yes, I will make the time. I will set aside a place for my dream. I will go for it. I will push through the litany of words that hold me back from achieving my true potential. I will seek out the joy of pursuing my dream despite the possibility of failure. I will push through the disappointments and letdowns until I emerge victorious.

Rewards and Positive Reinforcement—Even When You Don't Succeed

November 12, 2010

I didn't grow up in a household where there were a lot of rewards for good behavior. And we sure weren't rewarded for trying to be good either. So I came to this little idea of rewarding myself for not succeeding very slowly.

Apparently cleaning bathrooms after finishing a major project is not considered a reward. This is how well trained I was not to get something good even when I deserved it for all my hard work. But that is just stinky. Literally. Who wants to clean house after they've finished a paper, written a book, painted a picture, applied for graduate school, graduated from college, and the list goes on. I've learned to give myself breaks, but I had to teach myself to give myself rewards.

Kelly L. Stone articulated that precept for me at the GRW® Moonlight and Magnolias Conference® in Atlanta, Georgia. She gave me a few new ideas about how to reward myself while I am working toward a goal. I came home from the conference and implemented one. A successful author pays herself a quarter every time she meets her word count for the day. I decided to make a Reward Jar and got $20 in quarters to fill it.

Note: It'll take a lot of those rolls to fill my cutesy decorated tin can!

Any rate, I modified the reward system to include meeting every goal I set for the day as a writer (I might add exercise to that because I have been slacking off—which is a post for another day). So if my goal was to get a submission ready, a contest entry ready, a chapter read in my media book by Kristen Lamb, or my homework completed in an online workshop I'm taking, then I drop a quarter into the jar every time I meet the goal.

Another thing I've done is reward myself for having tried and failed. As a writer I must put myself out there all the time with query letters, sending out partials, full manuscripts and entering contests. I am not really into the administrative end of this business, so it is like poking a fork into my eyeball to do these things. I'd rather write my stories than do it. Seriously. But the work must be done. The possibility of rejections must be faced.

So here's how I cope. First, I get a quarter for completing the task. Then I devised a system for rewarding myself if I didn't get the answer I wanted (big yes or you finaled!). I pay myself for not getting those answers. Yup. Now these numbers can be adjusted to be coins, less money, more money, Hershey's kisses—you get the picture.

Here's my payment scale:

- Rejected Query? $1
- Rejected Partial? $5
- Rejected Full? $20
- Didn't Final in a Contest? $5
  (May 2015 Note: I still type for quarters and buy them back with twenty-dollar bills. It's a great motivator.)

Last week I didn't final in a contest. BOO. That stinks. I was down in the Personal Pity Party dumps. But then I remembered I got to pay myself $5 for not finaling. That brought a smile to my face. Yay! I put all the money I pay myself into a pretty box on a shelf in my office. It's up to you where you put your money (or Hershey's kisses). I am saving the quarters until I have too many to count, rolling them and putting them in the box.

What am I saving this money for? It's for anything to do with my writing—nice dress for an awards ceremony, shoes, dinner with writing friends, etc.

Now if you're not a writer and you're pursuing another goal or dream, you can modify this little reward system to suit your dream's not-so-happy days. For instance, if you are trying to get into university you can pay yourself for every application you send (a quarter cause those apps are expensive), for every study session you take for the SAT/ACT, for every interview you go on, for every college you tour, and for every good grade (say a B or better).

But hey? What if the college doesn't accept you? What will you pay yourself for trying so you'll try again? See? This system takes the sting out of not getting what you want and gives you motivation to try again.

Pay It Forward-Give Of Yourself Every Day

December 3, 2010

December has a Pay It Forward Day (at least that one pal on my Facebook says—so I'll roll with that info). I think it is a fabulous concept to carry in our hearts. However, I'd like to challenge all my friends and followers to have a Pay It Forward spirit throughout the year, every day, as we chug along and pursue our goals.

If we are able to pursue our goals, whatever they may be, then we are blessed. If we are educated, able to read, live in a country where freedom is a concept, not just a word, then we are blessed. If we have leisure time, can take time to read a book, cook a nice meal, break bread with friends and family then we are blessed.

If we can walk, talk, breath, sing, dance then we are blessed.

159

Yes, there are dark days. Yes, we all have tragedies that will occur in our lives. Yes, we will falter. But if we remember that we are truly blessed, we can carry that blessing into the world. This isn't a religious thing. This is a 'gee, gosh darn it you are bloody lucky and fortunate to live in a world where even having the time to read this book is a big deal.'

Seriously. It is.

So as you pursue your dreams, shoot for the moon, and grab for the stars, I hope you also remember to share yourself and Pay It Forward every day. Every day ask yourself what you are doing to make at least one person's life a bit better. I'm talking about strangers, people you meet in random ways, people you might never see again.

Many people want to accomplish big things and they go about changing the world. In big ways. That's great. That's wonderful. But if we can't practice kindness in small ways, we will never be tasked with big requests from the universe. Therefore I believe it is in the little acts of kindness that we truly evoke big changes in the world. A nice word, a friendly smile, a thank you, a compliment can go a long way to brighten a person's life. You never know how much of a difference one small act of kindness can cause. It is a ripple effect. The more ripples you gently stir into the waters of humanity, then the greater the waves of goodness will become in our world.

We don't have to shout out our good deeds or advertise them. We can be daily living examples of trying to live a life with purpose and kindness and compassion regardless of our religious beliefs, our backgrounds, or our cultures. So I encourage you to be aware of the people around you and to consciously and purposefully choose to act with kindness and compassion in your everyday encounters.

A New Year and A New Perspective: I'm a Professional

January 5, 2011

Every year I reflect upon my accomplishments before I set forth new goals and ideals for the New Year. This year I sat down to write my list of twenty-five accomplishments for the year and wrote over forty! Why so many? I wasn't just reflecting upon my work/writing accomplishments. No. I was reflecting upon my life and family accomplishments as a wife, a mother, and a friend.

I'm proud of all that I accomplished as a writer, but I am also very proud of my personal accomplishments. It's been an interesting year filled with challenges. The Physicist had a hip replacement surgery, I taught my daughter to drive, I said goodbye to my father-in-law, I hosted friends and family for visits, I traveled from here to NYC with my daughter on an epic road trip to tour colleges, I recommitted myself to building a community in my new city in Alabama, and I explored new places.

This was a great year.

As I sat down to renew my focus for 2011, I realized that with all the different hats I wear, I can no longer limit myself to just one set of five Top 5 Priorities. No. I am officially a full time writer with many goals, priorities, and commitments. There is also my personal life. I am a mother, a wife, and a friend. These areas of my life need to be separated and treated differently. Therefore, I see myself as a career writer who needs to organize her life accordingly.

I made two top 5 priority lists for this first quarter. Each list will be reviewed every quarter. Even better, the Physicist agrees that I need help with the household duties. I am 'working.' Now I have two master schedules. A schedule for writing and handling all the marketing/business/volunteer duties alongside my household schedule. The family minions, Darling Teen and the Physicist will help with household tasks.

It has happened. By taking myself seriously as a writer, and by gradually increasing my workload and my commitment to my dreams, I have become a professional career writer. Sure, I don't get paid (not unless you count the quarters I pay myself), but I am a professional. The proof is in the way my family and friends view me. I'm not just that lady who hauls her teen to voice lessons or who does laundry. Nope. I'm the 'writer in the family.'

I like it.

Self-respect. Taking myself seriously. It means being taken seriously by others. Try it this year. Respect your goals, your ambitions, your hopes, and your dreams. You might discover that others in your world do the same.

Life is a Roller Coaster, I Want to Ride It!

February 8, 2011

I rode my first roller coaster when I was 38 years old. I was forced into this crazy behavior by my daughter. She desperately wanted to ride THE BIG BAD WOLF® at Busch Gardens in Williamsburg®. I had to ride with her. I was sooooooooooooooooo scared! My only experience with roller coasters had been the tiny ones for little children, we're talking toddlers and grade school children, and that was fine with me. Why on earth would I want to hurl myself through loops and drops and corkscrews? Why? I loved my daughter and I wanted to give her the experience.

So on the coaster I went. And I fell in love with the thrill of the ride.

Oh, it was scary when we clickety-clacked up the track. I was so worried one or both of us would fall out of the cart. I think I checked my daughter's seatbelt a thousand and twenty times as we ascended. But, oh, the ride. The ride was so worth the fear! I was transported out of my worries, my problems, and the every day life events that can overwhelm a soul.

I was flying! I was so exhilarated by the experience that I quickly made my way through the list of the other rides at the theme park. Then I rode all the rides in Disney World®, Universal Studios® and Islands of Adventure®. One of my favorites is THE HULK®. Awesome ride.

I returned to the scene of my first coaster to ride THE GRIFFON®. Fear struck into my heart as I saw the people dangling face down, at a 90 degree angle, looking at the ground from high above the people gaping at them from below. Oh my goodness. I stood in the line, with my daughter and a family friend. My heart raced, my ears pounded with the thrumming belts of sheer terror. I didn't think I could ride this one. I wouldn't ride it. But onward ho. I walked all the way into the ride's entry. I sat down. My daughter held my hand. Our family friend held my other hand.

I didn't want to die. I was quite sure I would die on this ride. This was taking it too far.

We clacked up the track. I couldn't think. My brain squeezed with panic and I desperately wanted to get off the ride. I couldn't believe I'd done this ridiculous, stupid thing to myself. I let my daughter onto this beast. We were both going to die. I knew it.

Then we dangled, face first, suspended for mere seconds before we'd plummet to our death. The bird released and flew down the 90 degree drop. It was beyond anything I'd ever done. I wasn't just flying in a machine. I was the machine. I was a bird.

I loved it.

I endured the terror again 3 more times. Front, side on tip of wing, and back on other tip of wing.

The terror was worth the thrill of the ride.

The next time you're afraid to try something new, feel the fear and do it anyway. Do it for the thrill of the ride.

Realistically Impossible

March 1, 2011

I've been pondering the word *impossible* a lot these days.

Hmmmm. Why am I doing this? I do have a huge project looming so the word has marched into my mind a few times. How on earth can I possibly complete this task? Is it impossible for me to do what is necessary? What will I do with the information I have to transform what feels like an impossible task into a possible one? I've mulled the task. I've moaned about the task. I've danced around the task. I asked for encouragement about the task. I received support in super spades.

But it wasn't until I started the task that I realized that it was possible. Sometimes just starting a task means you will find a way to finish it even if you aren't sure how you will accomplish the end result.

Okay, that was easy enough. Start working and the impossible can become possible.

When I have power over the motion toward the goal, any task can become possible. Any task that doesn't require bungee cords, parachutes, trapezes, and a steady hand becomes possible. I've written about being realistic about setting goals. Not all of my goals were under my control. I knew when I posted the goals of 'get an agent and get an editor' that I was going to hear that I could only control how I pursued that goal.

I learned from a workshop presenter that it's okay to set these goals. They become imprinted in my mind and can transform my internal thought processes. Sure, I know these goals are realistically impossible for me to achieve on my own. I can't hogtie an agent or an editor and tell her/him to take me on as a writer. That wouldn't go over very well. But I can believe in the goals becoming a reality one day.

Writing them down gave me ownership over my belief.

The mere act of writing down the realistically impossible gave me a little burst of energy. It gave me power over my self-doubts. I developed a singularly strange inner confidence by sending my ultimate goals into the universe. I began to believe that all my goals were achievable. I was no longer constrained by the need to check them off my list in a timely manner. No. I was released from my inner demons of doubt and anxiety to do the other tasks that were necessary to achieving the realistically impossible.

Saying something can happen often, can make it happen. I don't know how this works. I just believe it does.

"There is no use in trying," said Alice; "one can't believe impossible things."

"I dare say you haven't had much practice," said the Queen. "When I was your age, I always did it for half an hour a day. Why, sometimes I've believed as many as six impossible things before breakfast." Lewis Carroll

I've dissected the word impossible and discovered this amazing fact:

I'm Possible.

(May 2015 Note: Long after I wrote this blog, I learned that Audrey Hepburn had a similar quote. She said, "Nothing is impossible, the word itself says 'I'm possible'!")

Smile and the World Smiles with You

January 13, 2012

I've had an admittedly weird and tough week. I tend to go through these every 3-4 months. January is pretty much a guaranteed month of mehness. It's cold. It's dark. It's gloomy. All the hype of Christmas is put up and the expectations of the New Year become insurmountable mountains to climb. How can I possibly get all these goals met? Why have I set the bar so high? Why do I continue to do this to myself?

It's like university all over again. I'd see the syllabus at the beginning of the semester and panic. How could I knock an A out of the park with this load of work? I'd procrastinate in fear of not being perfect. Then the fire would light in the form of a due date and I'd manage to squeak out the assignments.

I finished the degree with a 4.0 Summa Cum Laude and top of the Dean's List. Guess my technique worked for me.

So here I am in a mood, unable to concentrate on my writing goals other than judging and reading other people's writing or reading about writing knowing I have a lot of writing to do to keep the momentum going. What am I doing? I'm redecorating my media room, shopping for pretty baubles, avoiding my writing. Pretty typical mid-January for me!

Today I'm shopping and having fun with a friend. I'm waiting for information that could help me with my queries, and I'm thinking about my writing. I've decided to surrender to this weird state of inertia and share what makes me smile during this lunar phase of my life.

THINGS THAT MAKE ME SMILE

1. Tonks. That kitten has woven her way into my heart and is a joy. She makes us laugh with her antics and her naughty kittenish manners. She's sweet and cuddly or she's wild and crazy.
2. My writing friends. We laugh. We bring each other up and we manage to make light of this zany writing world. I could not survive being an unpublished writer if it weren't for them.
3. My non-writing friends. They show me there is more to the world than writing and help me find a happy heart by doing other non-writerly things like shopping and cooking and gossiping and just being.
4. Walt Disney®. I love him. I love his story. I love his vision. I am putting Disney® quotes in my media room. He's an amazing and inspirational man who understood that

adults are just children all grown up. We still want to play and laugh and sing.

5. Bright colors. I don't have many in the house right now. Taking down Christmas evaporated the cheer. I have a really cool ottoman with fabulous bright stripes. I am shopping for stuff that will pull those colors out of the ottoman and pop them in the rest of the family room, which is a tan shade and I thought I loved it when I bought the house, but I don't—too cheap to redo so shopping I go.

6. Reading. I love to read fiction and non-fiction. I go to books and magazines when I am blue. I'm reading a lot this week!!

7. Zumba and Pilates. I know exercise isn't always supposed to make one smile, but the ladies in my classes are fun, and I always leave the class in a better frame of mind than when I entered it. I love my classes.

8. Long walks and talks with good friends. I love to go on long 'jabber walks' and solve all the world's problems in an hour and a half.

9. Cooking. Cooking wonderful food and being in the kitchen is a creative and soulful outlet for me.

10. Entertaining. I love sitting around the dining room table with fun people and interesting people. The food is less important than the conversation.

So I'm doing the things that make me smile this week because I can't move past my inertia. It's okay. By Saturday/Sunday I'll be ready to hit the ground running again. But for this week and really during this gloomy month, I need to bring sunny events into my life or I won't be able to write well.

The Universe Speaks

January 16, 2013

Last weekend I had an icky kind of a Saturday/Sunday. Afterward I gave myself permission to rebel against my writing and just decorate the house, read other people's books and manuscripts, judge a contest, and hang out with friends.

The household and my non-writing friends benefitted from my mini-rebellion. I managed to get all kinds of fun things done for my media room and the living room. I got inspired by looking at baubles and trinkets and artwork. I read cool quotes, which I ordered as vinyl applications for my media room. By Saturday my well was full again.

I could feel myself easing back to the office, to my writing, to my daily grinding out of words and thoughts and emotions and actions. I was in a strange kind of a re-organization mood. First up? I had to get a new weight/measurement diary going. My old one was full and the last several weigh-ins/measurements had been done on sticky index post-its.

Never one to waste paper, I scrounged my writing office for a small journal to keep track of these measurements. I came across one that I had started as a 1000 things to be grateful for (stopped at 125, but I will add more) which also had quotes in it, randomly written jottings from *The Art of War for Writers* by James Scott Bell.

"Every moment spent whining about your writing career is a moment of creative energy lost... turn grousing into energy by writing!"

A clear reminder that whining about my writing and how slow the business side churns won't accomplish anything but valuable time wasted which could be used to be creative. Last week I couldn't face the computer. I channeled my energy into decorating the house because I could see a tangible result. I got one. Now I know what the universe expects of me. Quit worrying about the end game, just play it.

After that epiphany, I went into my office with a dust rag and furniture polish. I dusted all my pretty bookshelves from top-to-bottom until they gleamed. I threw away old papers and contemplated my writing. I looked at one shelf and opened my prayer jar—a small gift with scripture on it—in it was one slip of paper with 'That my books will one day be published' written in 2005. That slip of paper has been there for 7 years.

I refolded the paper, put it back inside the jar. Then in a frenzy of faith, I wrote out other prayers about my writing and my friends' writing and their dreams. Now the jar is full. Full of hope, faith, belief. Belief that one day my little slip of paper will be drawn out of that jar and a little hallelujah dance will occur because the prayer is answered.

When I looked at the order of books on the shelves, I discovered that I'd not put the writing books front and center. They were on lower shelves, parenting books were on the top shelf, and fiction books in the middle. The few writing craft and inspiration books I had were hidden behind pictures and doodads. Was I really taking my writing seriously? Really? Down deep at the gut level, at the subconscious emotional level where the mind works in wild and mysterious ways, I had not put the writing first.

I was clinging to old jobs or ways of thinking. I had how to parent and raise an optimistic child books front and center, but that job—while not finished—is clearly transitioning. I had my fun reading books in the center—yes they are pivotal to becoming a better writer, but they aren't about the business or craft per say.

I rearranged the shelves to reflect the changes and transitions in my life. The writing and craft books are front and center. I can see them and reach them easily.

The gorgeous picture of my daughter when she was 5 years old and precocious has moved to the top shelf because she is inspiration. That I— someone who had no strong foundation in life for parenthood—could raise a smart and beautiful and talented child to become a dreamer, an optimist, and an adventuring young woman is a rare gift.

She's proof that if I try hard enough, keep working on the weak and gray areas of this muddy mothering job, and persist in becoming as good an example of how to live and treat others, that than I can succeed. (Not that I did this alone—the Physicist has had a hand in all this but I like to think I was smart in choosing the best man for the future fathering job I had planned for him. LOL).

As I rearranged books, I came across a tiny blue gem that my dear CP and friend Sharon Wray sent to me last year as a gift. I think it was for my birthday so it's fitting that I come across it during my 'birthday week.' As always, I had put it into my shelf with the good intention of reading it when I had time and promptly forgot. But the Universe leads me to find things when I need them most. I picked up this tiny book *Gift from the Sea* by Anne Morrow Lindbergh (50th addition) and turned the pages to read.

Here's a quote that stirred my soul:

"The sea does not reward those who are too anxious, too greedy, or too impatient. To dig for treasures shows not only impatience and greed, but lack of faith. Patience, patience, patience, is what the sea teaches. One should lie empty, open, choiceless as a beach—waiting for a gift from the sea."

Now that needed to be read yesterday. Not sooner, not later. But yesterday. Today I am moving forward with a new direction. A new plan. A new spirit. I will probably never be the most patient person in the world (ask my CPs, the Physicist, the Teen—they'll readily concur), but I can always remind myself that I can't make it happen any faster by being anxious.

This leads me to my final quotes. Quotes that will go into the media room after they arrive.

"Around here, we don't look backwards for very long... we keep moving forward, opening up new doors and doing new things because we're curious... and curiosity keeps leading us down new paths."

"All our dreams can come true if we have the courage to pursue them."

Walt Disney®

I'm back. I'm ready to surge ahead. I'm moving forward with gusto and curiosity and faith. The universe has spoken to me and the message is loud and clear.

Who I Was Is Part of Who I Am and Who I Will Become

January 20, 2012

I have a saying to get through the bad days and moments which was 'It is what it is.' That's all well and good. It means I accept the circumstances for what they are and quit fighting. But that's not enough for me. I realized this week that I'm better off saying, "It will become what it will become—I will become who I become."

Then I realized that the past, mine in particular, has uniquely shaped me for the career I want to claim. My writing career is largely shaped by what I've overcome, learned, and will continue to learn. I used to think "if only I had not been sent on wild and crazy detours due to life, the circumstances I had to escape, and the education I had to delay, then I'd have started writing sooner."

Not anymore. I may not have an advanced university degree with all sorts of letters behind it, but I have something of equal or even greater value. I have a PhD in overcoming obstacles. Big ones for me, but not so big for others.

I'm so grateful for the lessons and emotions and experiences I've had because they shape the characters of my stories.

Here is a quick rundown:

- Born in the Netherlands to two people who survived Japanese Concentration camps in the 1940s. Neither of them were equipped to parent but they did the best they could.
- Canadian National Science Fair 3rd Place at 13 with project about Pattern Recognition.
- Figure skater for 8 years, alto sax player/second chair.
- Grew up in Northern mining town and experienced daily bouts of bullying because I 'used big words.'
- Semi-photographic memory, advanced reader, high IQ.
- Considered the *bad girl* in high school long before I did anything 'bad.'
- Smoker, back of the bleachers party girl, skipped school and forged my teachers' signatures on attendance sheets.
- Ran a mini-crime ring in forging teacher's names for other 'bad' kids—got caught.
- Spent 10th grade English in VPs office due to arguing a test question with teacher and winning my point.
- On my own at sixteen years old due to difficult home life.
- High school dropout.

- Worked in daycare, arena concession stand to make ends meet.
- Worked in diner.
- Waitress, gas jockey, maid.
- Drove without a license.
- Ice fished, snowmobiled, cross-country skied.
- Got my GED, learned how to sign for deaf/blind people in hope of going to college for free as interpreter.
- Lived in Northern Manitoba, Winnipeg, and Vancouver.
- Dated dangerous men, nice men, French men, Russian men, firemen, policemen, concert promoters, musicians and poets.
- Wrote poetry, loads and loads of it.
- Once wanted to be a foreign journalist.
- Once wanted to marry the Man from Atlantis—wrote an entire series about it long before fan fiction existed on the Internet.
- Read John Steinbeck, *The Hobbit*, *The Lord of the Rings* when I was in the 4th grade, reread them all later.
- Read Ginsberg, Kerouac and wished I'd been born in time to be a Beatnik.
- Kissed a French boy along the banks of the Seine when I was thirteen.
- Kissed the Physicist along the banks of the Seine when I was thirty.
- Married young, grew up with the Physicist, made a beautiful baby.

- Traveled to Europe, rode the Fast Train, been weighed on a witch's scale and deemed not a witch.
- My daughter and the Physicist believe I am strangely psychic—my dreams are often prophetic.
- I fly in my dreams. I want to fly in reality.
- I'm terrified of fire, drowning, death.
- I almost drowned on my first anniversary— the Physicist saved me.
- I was threatened by a bully with a cigarette lighter in the ninth grade. She wanted to burn my hair off my head. She had accomplices. I kicked her and ran away. She grew up and had a terrible life. I grew up and have a great life. Bad Karma is a bitch.
- I almost died 3 times due to anaphylaxis.
- I never wear a watch, but I have an uncanny awareness of time.
- The Physicist married me before I had a college degree. He didn't know I could cook, but I can.
- I graduated with a 4.0 Summa Cum Laude Bachelor of Science degree in Elementary Education at the top of the Dean's list.
- I never taught.
- I've worked in radio and television.
- I was a part-time model—I was the Sunshine Girl of West Vancouver.
- I have camped in the Redwood forest and in the Dordogne.

- When I make up my mind to do something, I just do it. If it becomes boring or routine I stop.
- Writing is the only thing that doesn't bore me.
- My paternal grandfather was a biologist for the World Health Organization as well as a practicing doctor.
- I got an A in pre-med genetics. Only two other people got As.
- I have an uncanny ability to diagnose diseases and illnesses.
- I'm more serious than people think I am.
- I'm more playful than people think I am
- I don't trust easily, but I am very trustworthy. If you tell me to keep a secret, I will. There are secrets I will die keeping.
- I believe in many truths. My main belief is do unto others as you would have done unto you. I have broken this rule as a young woman. I've seen others break it now. I wait for karma to act.
- I know what it is like to lose someone you love.
- I live here in the now, but I am not afraid to sift through the past for there is where real emotion, raw gritty emotion exists, the kind that can strengthen my stories and my characters.
- I play to win. Failure is not an option.
- If someone tries to stop me from winning out of spite, I will draw back, coil in my den, and wait to strike.

- Never mistake my desire to be kind as a weakness—never.
- I was once a dreamy, intellectual little girl who read big books and said big words because the mind was valued in our home.
- I was almost drowned in snow banks for being that little intellectual girl. I know what it is like to feel cold snow melting on your skin while you're desperately gasping for air and there is no one, no one to help you.
- A boy in the second grade used to chase me and punch me in the stomach daily. I put my book underneath my jacket and he punched me and broke his hand.
- I learned to be a *dumb blonde*.
- When I was in university, if you came up to me after a test, I could give you all the questions on the test verbatim as well as my answers.
- I worked as a night aide for a lady with Parkinson's disease. She told me her love story every time I came to sit with her. When I got engaged, she gave me her silver gravy boat that she had received for her wedding over 50 years earlier. I still have that gravy boat.
- I'm a dreamer, but I'm practical and serious. I believe in myself, but I also believe only hard work and tenacity will get me to where I want to go. But I WILL BECOME WHAT I WILL BECOME!!

If I, a person who started with so little could come so far and find such joy and a wealth of opportunities, then I'm proof that anyone with a little luck, some tenacity and brains, can succeed.

Follow your hearts, mine your pasts, and become who you will become.

YOLO: You Only Live Once

July 18, 2012

The Teen has a phrase: YOLO. It stands for You Only Live Once. She uses it quite a bit. It's a fun phrase to her and she lives life fairly happily. She's off to college in less than a month and I know she's ready.

I'll miss her, but I believe this will be an exciting transition for the entire family.

As part of my YOLO attitude, I've decided to feel the fear and go for it anyway. Yes, I've been afraid of failing at this writing gig more times than I can count: especially this year. I've wanted to quit numerous times. I was very full of doubt and despair, but I pushed through it with the help of my critique partners and writing friends.

There is no other option.

So my YOLO mantra will be about taking more chances as a writer. Trusting my heart and my instincts about the story and the characters.

Believing that if another writer can get published by my dream publishing line than I can, too.

It will happen.

So You Only Live Once. This year while my darling Teen heads to college to embrace her new adventure, I want to embrace mine. I'm a writer. Whether I get the call this year or next year, I am a writer. Whether I never get the call at all, I'm still a writer.

I do have control over many aspects of this career. I have a plan. The plan is in place. I am executing the plan at my pace and toward my goal. Other people might achieve their goals faster, or take shortcuts, but I am taking the road less traveled and sticking to my guns.

I want it all. That's it. YOLO.

Positively Realistic: Mining the Dark Side

July 20, 2012

I believe in living life to the fullest and in looking for the bright side of life, but the truth is that in order for me to be—and become—a strong writer with a story to tell, I must mine the dark side of life. I must look into dark corners. I must acknowledge the dark secrets all human beings carry in the depths of their souls. Only by paying homage to the dark side of life will I bring true depth to my stories.

Negativity ignored doesn't mean negativity doesn't exist. It does. In every person's heart and soul, regardless of the image cast upon the viewing world, there exists fears, doubts, concerns, secrets, dark memories. Even one of the most spiritual women I have admired throughout the years once confessed that in the still of the night she questioned the very existence of God. But then, in the morning, when she arose to do her charity work amongst the orphaned and diseased and deserted in India, she presented a positive and caring and devoted face.

This positivity thing is a choice. I applaud all who choose it. I try to be that person, but I cannot ignore the negativity of life nor can I avoid discussing it with other people—usually writers—because this darkness is what must be revealed if my readers are going to truly empathize with my characters.

I hope that in some way, by revealing my own doubt and despair throughout this journey through life that I am connecting with my readers in ways that will give them the strength to face their own dark secrets and overcome them.

After acknowledging the dark, we can then look for the light and be warmed by the hope it gives to all of us. It's there in every world religion, in every culture, in every human's heart. All people, all over the world, know universal truths that span the boundaries of distance and time. We are all connected by this global knowledge.

Pain, suffering, fears, doubts, pasts, secrets, love lost, love won, and the reality of death are not exclusive conditions. I cannot pretend they don't exist when I am mining my heart and soul as I build my characters and tell their stories.

And then when my characters overcome the dark chains of their pasts, when they reveal their innermost vulnerable selves to one another, when they grow to accept who they are and each other unconditionally, they receive the greatest reward. They receive the happily-ever-after they deserve.

Spider Solitaire and My Writing World

August 10, 2012

I have a confession. I like Spider Solitaire. I love the hardest version on my Nook. I play endless games of 4 deck Spider Solitaire. Sometimes I can tell pretty quickly whether I will win or not. I end the game early and start again. Other times it looks like I might have a chance, but alas, no. So I deal again. Every once in a while I win.

I win one game out of every gazillion tries. So why play? It's addictive. It empties my brain and for some reason that helps me with my writing. I LOVE it when I win. It's a wonderful, heady feeling to beat the game. To win and to have the little screen tell me I've won is awesome.

I play to win.

This Spider Solitaire is a lot like my writing world. It's been seven plus years. I've written eight books (some should never see the light of day). I've come close. Oh so close it hurts. But I haven't won yet. I can either give up altogether, or I can deal again.

I choose to deal again.

I had a great opportunity. I almost made it to the other side of the publishing world. Instead, I got a very nice letter about my book and my writing, about why it wouldn't fly with this line. Sadly, I agree with all the reasons the book won't fly. Won't lie. I was a bit down afterward.

But I got over it.

Why am I addicted to writing? I am addicted to solving the puzzle. I am addicted to the elusive idea of winning. I am so close to winning it hurts to come in second. I don't like hurting. I like winning. So guess what I'm doing?

I'm taking that letter's advice and suggestions to heart. They are the blueprint for the kind of books I want to write. They gave me encouraging words like 'promisingly high standards as a writer' and 'lots of things to love about your writing like...' And 'I'd be happy to read your next book's first three chapters.'

That's like getting a stacked deck, folks. That's a *you're so close that if you're willing to sit down and do all the work to understand and incorporate what we've suggested, then I will give you another chance because I LOVE MUCH ABOUT YOUR WRITING* kind of deck.

I like those odds. I like those words. I like this opportunity to break through.

Some people would give up. Some people would cave in under the weight of the pressure.

Some people would go elsewhere. Why don't I go somewhere else? Try some other publisher? Take a chance on me on my own? Why? I want my first published book to break out of the gate as a thoroughbred. I want my first published book to rush out of the gate and get to the front of the pack and be amazing and awesome and a *wow* book. I want my first book that gets published to land me readers who will ask, "Where has this author been my whole life because I want to read more of her books."

So that is why I am taking a break, reading a lot of books, making notes, taking time to think, think, think, and analyze the elements of these books. I am figuring out the final braiding of the pieces of the puzzle. I have everything I need in my toolbox to write a good book. Now I have the final puzzle piece. I have the elusive blueprint that will lead to my books becoming great.

Yeah, I'm that cocky. I'm that *on fire*. I'm that determined. I have to be this way or I will turn around and crawl back into my hole and hide. I will quit if I don't play to win.

I don't want to quit on myself. I want to take this opportunity and turn it into a winning hand of 4 Deck Spider Solitaire. I want to see that little screen pop up and say, "You Win!!"

Fate, Fortune Cookies, and Faith

June 5, 2013

I got what we writers like to say is *The Call.* In my case it was an email. I was sitting in my trusty Ford Escape® getting ready to go to my morning Zumba class when it arrived on my iPhone. So what did I do after my new editor at <u>Entangled Publishing</u> sent me the email that stated my manuscript was approved?

Frankly, I trembled. It was unbelievable, surreal even, after all these years of seeking a home for my stories.

I emailed her back—thanked her so much, and then I forwarded it to the Physicist and my critique partners, <u>Sharon Wray</u>, <u>Karen Johnston</u>, and <u>Pam Mantovani</u>. Sharon and Karen have worked with me since 2006 and they're talented writers whom I value beyond measure. Pam and I met through a contest that she was coordinating in 2009: the

Maggies® for the Georgia Romance Writers® RWA® Chapter. I finaled that year, and the following year I wooed her to become my category romance writing partner. We haven't looked back. She's an incredible writer, a fantastic critique partner, and a dear friend.

I would not be the writer I am today if fate had not lead me to these women. Our relationships are special and I love them all.

Fate also brought me to a fantastic writing group. The Romance Writers of America®. My first manuscript was requested by an editor at Harlequin and then rejected. Rightfully so. It was a hot mess and I needed to learn a lot. But in that rejection, the editor encouraged me to join RWA®. So I did. Then I found Karen and Sharon and then I found more writing chapters with my subsequent move to Alabama. Southern Magic®, Heart of Dixie®, Music City Romance Writers® and Georgia Romance Writers® have given me so much support throughout these long years.

Fate also led me to a fantastic group called GIAMx4 (Goal in a Month) after I emailed the loop's creator about a PRO post. Amy Atwell is a dynamo, and I adore her for including me in this group. They are so good to me.

Finally, fate also sent me a multi-published author who literally took me by the hand and said she'd read the first three chapters of the book I just sold because she knew how hard it is to get published. I finally plucked up the courage to send her this book and she fell in love with it. Though it didn't suit her publishing house's line, it did lead me down an interesting pathway. And her faith in my writing has kept me going when times got dark, and I wanted to give up writing for a shopping vocation.

But I couldn't quit writing. Then I would be—as Sharon so wisely and gently said—rejecting myself.

This brings me in no clear way to Fortune Cookies. For some reason I like saving certain fortunes that come in the cookies. I've kept two in my jewelry box for at least four years. I used one in my short bio because it suits me to a T. I kept the other one because it describes my internal motivation. Here they are:

- *Your ability to find the silly in the serious will take you far.*
- *Your skills will accomplish what the force of many will not.*

There were days when I'd open my jewelry box to get my hoop earrings and heart necklace and I'd read these fortunes just to jump start my day and keep my motivation going.

I came home and showed my daughter the email. She promptly hugged me three times in a row (a record!) and said she was proud of me. I still get all weepy when I recall that moment. Then it was off to PF Changs® because the day I sold to Entangled Publishing, the Physicist and I had already arranged a SWG with one of our favorite couples at the restaurant to catch up. SWG stands for Scotch Working Group. The servers there keep the Marine and the Physicist's favorite scotch on hand and know them by name. So one minute I was signing a contract and the next I was off to eat

Chinese and hang out with friends while my daughter started fooling around with my Tumblr account to make it look better.

When the Marine and his wife learned the news they were very excited. But really? I was so dazed. I was almost overwhelmed. They insisted on me tooting my own horn a bit. So we had a big piece of cake on the house (the server was happy for me after they told her I had sold a book). After we ate the cake (which was super yummy and completely sinful) the fortune cookies arrived. We each opened ours and I'm saving them all in my jewelry box. Here's what they said:

- *You will receive a surprising gift very soon.*
- *You should have a talk with a friend today.*
- *Treasure what you have.*
- *A small gift can bring joy to the whole family.*

Somehow, in the dim glow of the low lights at PF Changs® these fortunes reflected my entire day. I loved that moment when each member of the table read their slip of paper, then handed me their fortune.

Their friendship leads me to Faith. I could not have gotten to this point without the company of faithful friends and without faith in something greater than me guiding my destiny. My family, my dearest and oldest friends (two who read the first ill-fated manuscript and encouraged me to go forth), my new friends, my YMCA Sisters, my writing friends, my awesome critique partners, the mentors and teachers who have guided me, the published authors who have given me so much encouragement—all of them have filled my internal faith jar with hope for the future.

I have a real faith jar. Years ago someone gave me a prayer jar. You write down your prayers on slips of paper and date them, and then you put them in the jar and let them sit there. When things change, you check the jar and pull out the prayers that have been answered. OK, so now I'm crying as I write this because this weekend I pulled out two slips of paper. Here's what they said and the dates they were written:

- *I pray that someone will publish my works. 2005*
- *I pray for strength to write strong even when I'm not published. 2012*
- The top of my jar is inscribed with the following words:
- *Faith is the substance of things hoped for... Hebrews 11:1*

It's been a long journey from that first tiny slip of paper to today's new slip of paper. The journey's not over, it's just different. I'm making new connections and finding new friends who are in this extraordinary world that I've just entered. But I'm so glad that the companions I have known throughout my life will be cruising on this pathway beside me. They are why I have the courage to sit down to write stories that believe in the power of love binding two hearts together.

After *The Call*

May 2015

It's been two years since I received my *Call* to become a published author. Here's what's changed, and here's what has remained the same since that day.

What's changed isn't so much within me, but how people perceive me. I'm taken more seriously now when I share information about my writing process. Why? Somehow I am more credible because I'm a published author. But here's the thing: the wisdom that I acquired before I was published hasn't changed. It's still the same. But I'll take that gift and run with it just the same. I love helping other writers, published and unpublished and all across the board. My writing community is a constant source of inspiration and joy to me.

Another wonderful thing that's happened is that I've met the most amazing people—people who have read my books and have been moved by my words. I adore them. My critique partner Pam Mantovani and I have a Street Team called *The Passion Players* that makes being an author so much fun. I love the women on the team—their support and commitment to helping me get my name out there and be part of my publishing journey is beyond awesome.

Something else that has happened is that I'm not afraid to take a chance on myself. I've taken on the new challenge of becoming an independent author—Indie or Self Published authors have more control over their books and getting them into the readers' hands. I like that idea a lot! I still want to remain traditionally published, but I have learned that I can control the dream by championing my stories.

What remains the same is that I still struggle and battle with the Demons of Doubt and Despair. This is a tough business and there are a lot of ways one can get down about their writing. But I hang onto the words of other authors who say the minute you're confident, then you're done. A little fear is a good thing: it drives me to become a better writer.

That's the point. Becoming a better writer didn't end when I sold a book. If anything, I have strived to learn more and be stronger when I sit down to craft my stories. The books matter more than anything else I do now that I am a published author.

That's been the difficult part—finding time to write when I'm juggling all these new tasks like running a street team, promoting my books, developing workshops for writers, and connecting with my wonderful readers during personal appearances. But I do write because that is what is most important to me.

Now I have a publisher and an editor and my own ambition driving me to write compelling contemporary romances. Oh, I still have my days when I think maybe I should take a break and take up knitting wet noodles because that would be far easier than beating back the fear that I won't deliver another story that people might want to read.

But I won't stop. I can't stop. Writing is my passion. Learning the writing craft is my greatest challenge. I know that if I sit down every day to write, the universe will reward me for my effort. Not always in big ways, but the quiet voice of the muse talks and sends me solutions to all my story problems. I only have to listen with my heart.

Acknowledgements

My journey toward publication began as a solitary endeavor, but it soon transformed into one filled with many companions along the way. First, Sharon Wray and Karen M. Johnston took me under their wings and guided me. They encouraged me to join Romance Writers of America® and this professional organization has guided all my efforts in the years that I have been a member. Through RWA®, I have joined local romance writing chapters, attended writing conferences, taken online classes, and have been mentored. I am honored to be part of such a wonderful group of writers who genuinely encourage people to attain their dream to become a published romance novelist.

I owe a big super thanks to my critique partner, Pam Mantovani. Thanks for the picky alerts, the wine, the laughter, and the support my friend!! I would not be the writer I am today without your input and advice. I am so glad we're sharing this special time in our lives.

Thank you to my very first editor, Alethea Spiridon Hopson at Entangled Publishing, LLC. She believed in my story *The Maverick's Red Hot Reunion* and in it's prequel *The Movie Star's Red Hot Holiday Fling.* Now we're working together on a new story for Entangled Publishing. She's a wonderful editor, and I am lucky to have had the privilege of working with her. I'm also very grateful for editor Kate Fall who took my writing to the next level with her probing questions and insight into the characters and their motivations. Everyone at Entangled deserves a huge shout out: the copy editors, proof readers, cover artists and business staff have been awesome throughout this journey.

My family is my greatest support network. Chuck, AKA the Physicist, has to listen to all my writing woes and worries. Mallory has become the romance writers' official right hand girl with her graphic designs, website designs, and ongoing creative endeavors to make me and my friends look really super online and in person. Thanks to both of you for putting up with the down days and cheering for me during the high days.

My friends—Lori, Heidi, Janne Marieke, Petra, and all of the fabulous people in my world—have been instrumental in keeping me sane, mostly with wine and laughter and love. Y'all make me want to go out there and do the things I do. You enrich me in ways that are immeasurable. I love you.

Mucho thanks to my and Pam's Street Team!! *The Passion Players* are the best team I could ask for as an author. Thanks for the support, the virtual wine, the Man Candy, and the laughter. You make what I do so much fun!! I heart you all!!

Thanks to every writer and reader who has touched my life. I wish you all the highest of heights and the greatest of accomplishments. Follow your passion and live joyfully!!

Christine's Books

The Tycoon's Red Hot Marriage Merger
Sweetbriar Springs Series from Entangled Publishing
The Movie Star's Red Hot Holiday Fling-Book One
The Maverick's Red Hot Reunion-Book Two
Coming soon from Entangled Publishing
The Italian Tycoon's Marriage Bargain

Want to keep up with my upcoming releases and other fun news? Join my newsletter here http://eepurl.com/L8Yh5

I love to connect with people online and in person. Here's some fun ways to find me:
Email: christinegloverauthor@gmail.com
Facebook Page: https://www.facebook.com/pages/Christine-Glover/158387587541698

Passion Players Street Team: https://www.facebook.com/groups/14853656 51680656/

Twitter: https://twitter.com/cjglover63

Tumblr: http://christinejhglover.tumblr.com

Pinterest: http://www.pinterest.com/cjglover63/

Google+: https://plus.google.com/u/1/+Christine Gloverauthor

website: www.christinegloversite.com

Author Goodreads: https://www.goodreads.com/author/sho w/8294375.Christine_Glover

About Christine

Born in the Netherlands, Christine moved to Canada where she spent her formative years. Then she married her Texan Alpha Physicist, moved to the United States and she has lived both south and north of the Mason Dixon line. Now Christine resides in Alabama with her husband, two insane cats and her wonderful daughter. She enjoys finding the silly in the serious, making wine out of sour grapes, and giving people giggle fits along with heartfelt hugs. When she's not writing, you can find her traveling the world, cooking gourmet food, and desperately seeking a corkscrew.

Glossary of Terms

- CP: Critique Partner
- DDJ: Dreaded Day Job
- DNJ: Dreaded Night Job
- FIL: Father-in-law
- GH: Golden Heart® Contest for Unpublished Writers
- GMC: Goal, Motivation, & Conflict
- GRW: Georgia Romance Writers®
- HOD: Heart of Dixie® RWA Chapter
- M&M: Moonlight & Magnolias Conference presented by the Georgia Romance Writers®
- MS: Manuscript
- NYT: New York Times
- POV: Point of View
- PPP: Pivotal Plot Point or Personal Pity Party
- PRO: A status attained as career focused writer within the RWA® that emphasizes completion of a romance novel or novella

- R: Rejection
- R&R: Revise and resubmit
- RS: Romantic Suspense
- RWA: Romance Writers of America®
- ST: Single Title
- WIP: Work in Progress
- YA: Young Adult

Author Note: If you are reading a paperback version of this book, the underlined names and underlined book titles indicate hyperlinks to their websites and book sale information.

Cited Sources

Arnot, M.D., Robert. *The Biology of Success*, Published 2000 Little, Brown and Company.

Bell, James Scott. *The Art of War for Writers: Fiction Writing Strategies, Tactics, and Exercises,* Published 2009 Writer's Digest Books. (http://www.jamesscottbell.com/)

Buckham, Mary and Love, Dianna. *Break into Fiction: 11 Steps to Building a Story that Sells*, Published 2009 Adams Media/Avon. (http://marybuckham.com/ & https://www.authordiannalove.com/)

Maass, Donald. *Writing the Breakout Novel*, Published 2001 Writer's Digest Books. (http://maassagency.com/)

Lindbergh, Anne Morrow. *The Gift from the Sea.* First published 1955, renewed 1975, and renewed 1983 Pantheon Books, a division of Random House Publishing.

Richardson, Cheryl. *Life Makeovers,* Published 2000 Broadway Books, a division of Random House Publishing. (http://www.cherylrichardson.com/)

Writing Craft Resources

The following is a list of books and other writing resources that have guided my writing journey and my understanding about the craft:

Ackerman, Angela and Puglish, Becca. *The Emotion Thesaurus: A Writer's Guide to Character Expression*, Published 2012 Cyber Witch Press. (www.thebookshelfmuse.blogspot.com)

Bell, James Scott. *Plot & Structure*, Published 2004 Writer's Digest Books. (http://www.jamesscottbell.com/)

Bell, James Scott. *Revision & Self-Editing*, Published 2008 Writer's Digest Books. (http://www.jamesscottbell.com/)

Cowden, Tami D., LaFever, Caro, Viders, Sue. *The Complete Writer's Guide to Heroes & Heroines: Sixteen Master Archetypes*, Published 2000 Watson-Guptill Publications, an imprint of the Crown Publishing Group.

Dixon, Debra. *Goal, Motivation & Conflict: The Building Blocks of Good Fiction*, Published 1996 Gryphon Books for Writers.

Kenyon, Sherrilyn. *Character Naming Sourcebook: Second Edition.* Published 2005 Writer's Digest Books, an imprint of F+W Publications, Inc.

King, Stephen. *On Writing: A Memoir of the Craft*, Published 2000 Scribner a division of Simon & Schuster.

Kipfer, Barbara Ann, Ph.D. *Flip Dictionary: For When You Know What You Want to Say But Can't Think of the Word.* Published 2000 Writer's Digest Books, an imprint of F+W Publications, Inc.

Pressfield, Steven. *The War of Art*, Published 2002 Black Irish Entertainment LLC.

Pressfield, Steven. *Turning Pro: Tap Your Inner Power and Create Your Life's Work*, Published 2012 Black Irish Entertainment LLC.

Rodale, J.I. *The Synonym Finder*, Published 1978 Grand Central Publishing.

Snyder, Blake. *Save the Cat: The Last Book On Screenwriting That You'll Ever Need*, Published 2005 Sheridan Books, Inc.

Useful Websites & Other Information

http://marybuckham.com/
http://www.storymastery.com/
http://www.margielawson.com/
https://www.rwa.org/
http://authorkellylstone.com/
http://www.christophervogler.com/
https://warriorwriters.wordpress.com/